COMPACT *Research*

Drug Legalization

Current Issues

ReferencePoint Press™

San Diego, CA

Other books in the Compact Research series include:

Current Issues
Abortion
Biomedical Ethics
Cloning
The Death Penalty
Energy Alternatives
Free Speech
Global Warming and Climate Change
Gun Control
Illegal Immigration
Islam
National Security
Nuclear Weapons and Security
Obesity
School Violence
Stem Cells
Terrorist Attacks
U.S. Border Control
Video Games
World Energy Crisis

Diseases and Disorders
Anorexia
Autism
Hepatitis
Meningitis
Phobias
Sexually Transmitted Diseases

Drugs
Alcohol
Club Drugs
Cocaine and Crack
Hallucinogens
Heroin
Inhalants
Marijuana
Methamphetamine
Nicotine and Tobacco
Performance-Enhancing Drugs
Prescription Drugs

COMPACT *Research*

Drug Legalization

by Peggy J. Parks

Current Issues

ReferencePoint
Press™

San Diego, CA

Picture credits:
Maury Aaseng: 35–38, 52–55, 68–71, 85–88
AP Images: 15, 18

Parks, Peggy, J.
  Drug legalization / by Peggy J. Parks.
    p. cm.—(Compact research series)
  Includes bibliographical references and index.
  ISBN-13: 978-1-60152-012-8 (hardback)
  ISBN-10: 1-60152-012-3 (hardback)
  1. Drug legalization—United States. 2. Drug control—United States. I. Title.
  HV5825.V34 2008
  363.450973—dc22   2007016582

Contents

Foreword

"Where is the knowledge we have lost in information?"

—"The Rock," T.S. Eliot.

As modern civilization continues to evolve, its ability to create, store, distribute, and access information expands exponentially. The explosion of information from all media continues to increase at a phenomenal rate. By 2020 some experts predict the worldwide information base will double every 73 days. While access to diverse sources of information and perspectives is paramount to any democratic society, information alone cannot help people gain knowledge and understanding. Information must be organized and presented clearly and succinctly in order to be understood. The challenge in the digital age becomes not the creation of information, but how best to sort, organize, enhance, and present information.

ReferencePoint Press developed the *Compact Research* series with this challenge of the information age in mind. More than any other subject area today, researching current issues can yield vast, diverse, and unqualified information that can be intimidating and overwhelming for even the most advanced and motivated researcher. The *Compact Research* series offers a compact, relevant, intelligent, and conveniently organized collection of information covering a variety of current topics ranging from illegal immigration and methamphetamine to diseases such as anorexia and meningitis.

The series focuses on three types of information: objective single-author narratives, opinion-based primary source quotations, and facts and statistics. The clearly written objective narratives provide context and reliable background information. Primary source quotes are carefully selected and cited, exposing the reader to differing points of view. And facts and statistics sections aid the reader in evaluating perspectives. Presenting these key types of information creates a richer, more balanced learning experience.

For better understanding and convenience, the series enhances information by organizing it into narrower topics and adding design features that make it easy for a reader to identify desired content. For example, in *Compact Research: Illegal Immigration*, a chapter covering the economic impact of illegal immigration has an objective narrative explaining the various ways the economy is impacted, a balanced section of numerous primary source quotes on the topic, followed by facts and full-color illustrations to encourage evaluation of contrasting perspectives.

The ancient Roman philosopher Lucius Annaeus Seneca wrote, "It is quality rather than quantity that matters." More than just a collection of content, the *Compact Research* series is simply committed to creating, finding, organizing, and presenting the most relevant and appropriate amount of information on a current topic in a user-friendly style that invites, intrigues, and fosters understanding.

Drug Legalization at a Glance

Illicit Drugs

A number of drugs are illegal in the United States, including cannabis, which is used to make marijuana and hashish; cocaine and heroin; methamphetamine; and hallucinogens such as LSD and ecstasy.

Prevalence

As of 2006 an estimated 20.4 million Americans aged 12 or older used drugs regularly. Marijuana was the most prevalent drug, followed by cocaine, methamphetamine, heroin, and hallucinogens.

Drug Laws

The Drug Enforcement Administration (DEA) enforces drug laws in the United States. The Controlled Substances Act gives the federal government jurisdiction over all drug offenses, although states also have their own laws in place.

Drugs and Crime

According to the DEA, more than half of all people arrested for violent crimes are under the influence of drugs when they commit the crimes.

Incarceration Rate

Tougher drug laws in the United States have led to a significant rise in incarcerations: In 1970 the prison population was 196,429, but by 2007 it had climbed to more than 2 million.

Drug Laws and Addiction

An estimated 125 million Americans are regular alcohol drinkers, compared to 20.4 million regular drug users. Legalization opponents say that if drugs became legal, more people would become addicted.

The War on Drugs

The war on drugs began in 1971 when President Richard Nixon first used the term. Since that time, an estimated $500 billion has been spent on fighting drug use.

Overview

The word *drug* applies to everything from the caffeine contained in coffee and chocolate to over-the-counter medicines such as cough syrup, aspirin, and Tylenol. But when people talk about legalization, they are referring to illicit substances such as marijuana, cocaine, heroin, methamphetamine, and hallucinogens, all of which are illegal in the United States, Canada, and a number of other countries.

Marijuana, often called "weed" or "pot," is the most commonly used illegal drug. According to the 2006 National Survey on Drug Use and Health (NSDUH), nearly 98 million Americans 12 years of age or older said they had tried it at least once in their lifetimes. Marijuana comes from the cannabis plant, which grows wild throughout most of the tropic and temperate regions of the world. The leaves and flowering tops of the plant are dried to produce a tobacco-like substance that is smoked in a pipe or rolled into a cigarette known as a joint. Cannabis contains a

Overview

number of psychoactive compounds, the most potent of which is delta-9-tetrahydrocannabinol, better known as THC.

Cocaine, which is extracted from the leaves of the coca plant, may either be a white crystalline powder that is snorted into the nostrils or in a rock-like form, known as crack cocaine, that is smoked in a pipe. Heroin, another drug of natural origin, is derived from the seedpods of a certain species of poppy. Although poppies are grown all over the world, most heroin in the United States comes from Colombia, Mexico, Southeast Asia, and Southwest Asia (principally Afghanistan). Traditionally heroin was dissolved, diluted, and then injected into a user's vein using a syringe, but the Drug Enforcement Administration (DEA) says that a growing percentage of today's users are either snorting or smoking heroin.

Unlike cannabis, cocaine, and heroin, some illegal drugs are synthetic and manufactured in clandestine laboratories. Methamphetamine (meth) is part of a group of drugs known as amphetamines, and may either be injected or smoked. Also manufactured in laboratories are drugs such as LSD, PCP (angel dust), and ecstasy, all of which are hallucinogens, or psychoactive drugs that distort perceptions and can cause hallucinations.

How Drugs Affect the Body

Drugs have different effects depending on the substances they contain. The THC in marijuana attaches to brain receptors that are involved in pleasure, appetite regulation, and perception of pain. Its effect is similar to that of alcohol; people who smoke it typically experience feelings of fuzzy mellowness and general well-being. Many people insist that marijuana is no more harmful than alcohol, but according to the DEA, it contains a number of toxins and cancer-causing chemicals. Extended use can potentially damage the lungs and reproductive system, as well as interfere with the immune system's ability to function properly. The DEA claims that chronic, long-term use of marijuana has been associated with a disorder known as amotivational syndrome, which is characterized by impaired judgment, memory, and concentration, as well as an overall sense of apathy toward appearance, pursuit of goals, and life in general.

Like marijuana, heroin can also induce feelings of dreamy drowsiness and a general sense of well-being, along with a rush of euphoria. Once heroin is in the body, it quickly enters the brain and latches onto opioid receptors. Opioids are naturally produced by the body and influence hunger, thirst, and moods, as well as regulate the immune system. Because heroin is an artificial opioid, it mimics natural opioids and can completely change how a user feels. The greatest danger of heroin, however, is that users can overdose on it, which can result in respiratory failure and death.

Cocaine has a very different effect on the body than marijuana or heroin. It is an "upper," a drug that increases heart rate and blood pressure and rapidly induces feelings of exhilaration, energy, and self-confidence. The intensity of cocaine's effects depends on the dose and how the user ingests it. When it is snorted, it reaches the brain in 3 to 5 minutes, while intravenous injection produces a rush in 15 to 30 seconds—yet these exhilarating effects are often short-lived. After anywhere from 15 minutes to an hour, a cocaine high wears off and will likely be followed by extreme fatigue and sadness. The DEA refers to this as a "dysphoric crash" and explains what often follows and the associated risks: "To avoid the fatigue and the depression of coming down, frequent repeated doses are taken. Excessive doses of cocaine may lead to seizures and death from respiratory failure, stroke, or heart failure."[1]

> " Marijuana, often called 'weed' or 'pot,' is the most commonly used illegal drug. "

The effects of methamphetamine, another powerful stimulant, are similar to cocaine, but their onset is slower. And because meth remains in the central nervous system longer than cocaine, its effects are felt for a longer period of time. Meth disrupts transporters of dopamine, which is an essential chemical in the brain that regulates movement, emotion, motivation, and feelings of pleasure. When people take meth, their brains are flooded with abnormally high levels of dopamine, the effects of which are explained by the National Institute on Drug Abuse (NIDA): "This disruption produces a greatly amplified message. . . . The difference in effect can be described as the difference between someone whispering into your ear and someone shouting into a microphone."[2] Meth causes heart rate and blood pressure to soar, and users feel overcome with pleasure, often feeling powerful and even invincible. This high lasts for about 16 hours; afterward, aggression and paranoia begin to creep up alongside the pleasure. The DEA says that chronic use of meth can lead to psychosis that resembles schizophrenia and can result in violent, erratic behavior.

Hallucinogens such as LSD and ecstasy also cause elevated heart rate and increased blood pressure. The effects of these drugs can vary based on the dose and the user's mood but typically include feelings of euphoria and increased energy, followed by distorted thoughts and rich, vivid hallucinations. One side effect of LSD is flashbacks; users have reported having sudden hallucinogenic episodes days or even months after taking it. Ecstasy is an even riskier drug; regular users can sustain damage to nerve cells that can lead to permanent brain damage. The DEA describes ecstasy by saying it "short-circuits" the body temperature signals to the brain. This can cause someone's body temperature to rise to as much as 117 degrees Fahrenheit (47.2 degrees Celsius), leading to severe dehydration or heat stroke. The drug can also have the opposite effect, causing body temperature to plummet, which can lead to hypothermia and permanent organ damage, seizures, stroke, and death.

Drug Addiction

Most drugs have the potential to be addictive, but some are more addictive than others. Whether users can become addicted to marijuana is a major subject of controversy. The NIDA says that it is addictive because frequent, heavy marijuana users develop a tolerance to the drug's effects. In other words, the longer they use it, the more of it they need to get the same high they used to get from smaller amounts. Amy Hughes, a young woman from western Michigan who used to smoke marijuana every day, says that personal experience leads her to agree with the NIDA. Although she says it may differ from person to person, she believes she had become addicted, and it frightened her. She says:

> At first, all it took was a few puffs for me to get high. But as time went by a few puffs didn't cut it anymore, didn't have any effect. So I smoked more pot, and still more. Finally I got to the point where I was rushing home from work every single day because I couldn't wait to get high. I felt like it was starting to dominate my life, so I quit. Now I smoke it maybe a couple times a year, and I don't miss the habit.[3]

According to a report by the Substance Abuse and Mental Health Services Administration (SAMHSA), 22.6 million Americans suffer from substance dependence or abuse problems. Whether addiction occurs depends on a number of factors, including biology (genetics, gender, and mental disorders); environment (home life, parents' use and attitudes, and influence of peers); and the properties and effects of the drug itself. Another factor is age; in general, people who start using drugs when they are adolescents are more likely to become addicted because their brains have not yet fully developed.

Should Certain Drugs Be Legalized?

Whether drugs should be legalized is a hotly debated issue. Some who are in favor of drug legalization believe that all drugs should be legalized, controlled by the federal government, and taxed, in the same way that alcohol and tobacco products are handled today. That is the perspective of Kailash Chand, a physician from the United Kingdom, who explains: "Many people may think that taking drugs is inherently wrong and so should be illegal. But there is a question of effectiveness—does making it illegal stop people doing it? The answer is clearly no. One could even argue that legalisation would eliminate part of the attraction of taking drugs—the allure of doing something illegal."[4]

Other drug legalization advocates believe that only so-called soft drugs such as marijuana should be legalized. Stan Kid, who is a lieutenant with the Malverne Police Department in Long Island, New York, favors legalization of some drugs as long as there is strict quality control in drug manufacturing. "I don't know that marijuana is any more or less than alcohol use or misuse," he says, "but I believe most of the heavy-duty drugs should continue to be banned (heroin, crack cocaine, etc)."[5]

Would Legalizing Drugs Decrease Crime?

A common argument on behalf of drug legalization is that violent crime associated with illegal drugs is primarily fueled by drug trafficking; that is, crime is a by-product of the buying and selling of drugs on the black market. If drugs became legal, advocates say, drug-related crime and violence would markedly decrease. Chand shares his view on this: "A sensible policy of regulation and control would reduce burglary, cut gun crime, bring women off the streets, clear out our overflowing prisons, and raise

In this marijuana bust in Arizona, 45 bundles of marijuana, weighing about 25 pounds each, were recovered. As of 2006 an estimated 20.4 million Americans aged 12 or older used drugs regularly. Marijuana was the most commonly used drug.

billions in tax revenues."[6] The DEA disagrees, saying that violent offenders are most dangerous when they take drugs. The agency adds that six times as many homicides are committed by people under the influence of drugs than by those who are looking for money to buy drugs.

Would Legalizing Drugs Increase Drug Addiction?

Those opposed to drug legalization are convinced that if illicit drugs were readily available, the number of drug addicts would soar. Research by SAMHSA shows that the number of people who abuse alcohol is more than 6 times higher than the number of illicit drug users. Legalization opponents are especially concerned about young people; in 2006, nearly

11 million youths aged 12 to 20 reported that they had drunk alcohol in the past month and 2.4 million said that they were heavy drinkers. If drugs became legal, these young substance abusers could easily be at risk for abusing drugs as well as alcohol.

Legalization advocates argue that making drugs legal would have little or no effect on drug addiction. In their view, people who want to take drugs, and subsequently become addicted to drugs, are not dissuaded by current drug laws; whether drugs are legal or not, users will find a way to get them. British author and philosophy professor A.C. Grayling writes: "Almost everyone who wishes to try drugs does so; almost everyone who wishes to make use of drugs does it irrespective of their legal status. Opponents say legalisation will lead to unrestrained use and abuse. Yet the evidence is that where laws have been relaxed there is little variation in frequency or kind of use."[7]

> "The DEA says that chronic use of meth can lead to psychosis that resembles schizophrenia and can result in violent, erratic behavior."

In December 2007 StoptheDrug War.org released a public opinion poll that involved 1,028 adults 18 years of age and older. When asked, "If hard drugs such as heroin or cocaine were legalized, would you be likely to use them?" 99 percent of the respondents answered no. According to David Borden, the organization's executive director, the survey results indicate that drug legalization would not necessarily have an effect on addiction.

The War on Drugs

In 1970 the U.S. Congress passed the Controlled Substances Act. This was a powerful piece of legislation because for the first time in American history, federal jurisdiction was asserted over all drug offenses, no matter how small or local in scope. The following year President Richard Nixon coined the term "war on drugs" to describe his get-tough approach toward eradicating the problem of illegal drug use in the United States. In 1972 Nixon signed into law the Drug Abuse Office and Treatment Act, which he described as mounting "a frontal assault on our number one public enemy" that was designed to "wipe out drug abuse in America."[8] Within a year Nixon had created the DEA, and in 1982, when Ronald Reagan was president, Congress mandated the creation of a "drug czar" to oversee the country's battle against illegal drugs.

> Legalization advocates argue that making drugs legal would have little or no effect on drug addiction.

Although Nixon and Reagan stepped up the drug control effort, drug laws had already been in place for many years before either of them took office. The Harrison Narcotics Tax Act, passed by Congress in December 1914, was intended to ensure the orderly marketing of narcotics. It provided that manufacturers, importers, pharmacists, and physicians who prescribed narcotics to their patients should be licensed to do so for a moderate fee. The law was not originally written to prohibit drugs. But because of a clause that stated "in the course of his professional practice only,"[9] law enforcement officers began cracking down on physicians who prescribed narcotics for patients who were addicts. Those who continued to do so risked being arrested, and some were convicted and sent to prison. Over the years the Harrison Narcotics Tax Act continued to be tightened until it evolved into full-scale prohibition legislation. In 1937 the Marijuana Tax Act added cannabis to the list of outlawed substances.

Today, the war on drugs continues, with as much as $50 billion federal, state, and local dollars spent each year to fight the use of illegal substances. Tens of thousands of federal, state, and local law enforcement officials currently work full-time on drug-related assignments.

Is It the Government's Place to Regulate Drugs?

The DEA, as well as many government leaders, argue that tough laws are necessary in order to protect people from escalating drug use and addiction. In defending his administration's drug control strategy, President George W. Bush stated in February 2008 that the government's efforts were "inspired by a great moral imperative" and that "we must reduce illegal drug use because, over time, drugs rob men, women, and children of their dignity and of their character."[10] Yet the question legalization advo-

A woman in the Netherlands harvests hallucinogenic mushrooms in a growing room. Effects of hallucinogenic drugs can vary based on the dose and the user's mood but typically include feelings of euphoria and increased energy, followed by distorted thoughts and rich, vivid hallucinations.

cates often ask is, by keeping drugs illegal, is the federal government trying to play nanny?

During a 1991 interview, the late Milton Friedman, a Nobel Prize–winning economist who was a staunch supporter of drug legalization, stated that the government had no business trying to protect people from themselves. He said:

> The case for prohibiting drugs is exactly as strong and as weak as the case for prohibiting people from overeating. We all know that overeating causes more deaths than drugs do. If it's in principle OK for the government to

say you must not consume drugs because they'll do you harm, why isn't it all right to say you must not eat too much because you'll do harm? Why isn't it all right to say you must not try to go in for skydiving because you're likely to die? Why isn't it all right to say, "Oh, skiing, that's no good, that's a very dangerous sport, you'll hurt yourself"? Where do you draw the line?[11]

Authors David Boaz and Timothy Lynch share Friedman's viewpoint. In their *Cato Handbook for Congress: Policy Recommendations for the 108th Congress*, they explain that there are numerous reasons why Congress needs to repeal the Controlled Substances Act of 1970, abolish the DEA, and end the current war on drugs. Boaz and Lynch maintain that federal drug laws are "constitutionally dubious" because the Tenth Amendment grants powers to the states or to the people, which means the federally led war on drugs is unconstitutional. They write:

> The United States has a tradition of individual liberty, vigorous civil society, and limited government. Identification of a problem does not mean that the government ought to undertake to solve it, and the fact that a problem occurs in more than one state does not mean that it is a proper subject for federal policy. Perhaps no area more clearly demonstrates the bad consequences of not following such rules than does drug prohibition.[12]

Do Drug Arrests Unfairly Target Minorities?

Many people are convinced that the enforcement of current drug laws is decidedly biased against minorities. Based on statistics from the U.S. Census Bureau, the American population was just over 300 million people in 2006, of which 66 percent (200 million) were Caucasians and 13 percent (40 million) were African Americans. The Centers for Disease Control and Prevention (CDC) reports that current illicit drug use in 2006 among white users 12 years of age or older was 8.5 percent, or roughly 17 million people, while drug use among blacks of the same age group was 9.8 percent, or 3.9 million people. Department of Justice statistics for 2006 show that 875,000 whites and 484,000 blacks were

> **" Since 1999 the use of illegal drugs in the United States has risen nearly 40 percent, which has caused many people to conclude that the war on drugs is failing miserably. "**

arrested for drug-related offenses. Thus, while 4 times as many drug users were white, the arrest rate of black users was nearly 150 percent higher than that of whites. Also, a disproportionate number of minorities are imprisoned on drug-related charges. A December 2007 report by the Bureau of Justice Statistics shows that in 2004, 65,900 white people were incarcerated for drug offenses compared with 112,500 African Americans. In a 2006 report by the American Civil Liberties Union, black drug users were shown to represent 50 percent of those convicted and 74 percent of all drug offenders sentenced to prison. As journalist Arianna Huffington writes: "Consider this: The U.S. has 260,000 in state prisons on nonviolent drug charges; 183,200 (more than 70%) of them are black or Latino."[13]

Is the War on Drugs Failing?

Since 1999 the use of illegal drugs in the United States has risen nearly 40 percent, which has caused many people to conclude that the war on drugs is failing miserably. As Boaz and Lynch write: "The long federal experiment in prohibition of marijuana, cocaine, heroin, and other drugs has given us crime and corruption combined with a manifest failure to stop the use of drugs or reduce their availability to children."[14] One of the most contentious arguments in the drug legalization battle is over the arrest and/or imprisonment of users who are nonviolent offenders and present no harm to society, particularly with regard to marijuana. Although states may set their own guidelines for punishment, federal law calls for a year in jail and a $1,000 fine for anyone who is caught with marijuana, no matter how small the quantity. In 38 states, even first-time offenders possessing a small amount of marijuana can be imprisoned. According to journalist Gary Cartwright, 97 percent of all marijuana arrests are for possession of an ounce (about 28g) or less. Another consideration is that the war on drugs was intended to drive up drug prices so people would not be able to afford them, but this has not happened. In 1981 the price of a pure gram (about 0.04 ounces) of cocaine was roughly $600; by 2005, the price had dropped to around $135. The cost of heroin, ecstasy, and marijuana has also decreased over the years.

Although the DEA acknowledges that the current war on drugs has room for improvement, it argues that the effort must continue. The agency reports it has had many successes in the fight against illicit drug use; for example, even though more than 20 million Americans still use illegal drugs, that number has decreased since 1979, when there were an estimated 25 million drug users. Also, the use of illicit drugs by American teenagers has steadily declined since the mid-1990s, from 24 percent in 1996 to 13 percent by 2007. "Progress does not come overnight," says the DEA. "America has had a long, dark struggle with drugs. . . . Now is not the time to abandon our efforts"[15]

Should Certain Drugs Be Legalized?

66The scariest word for those who profit in the black market of drugs is 'legalization.' That's a word they don't want to hear. They know that as long as drugs are illegal they will have a tax-free, golden egg laying goose.99

—Russ Jones, "War on Drugs Is a Lost Cause."

66We emphatically disagree with those who favor drug legalization. Drug legalization would be a social catastrophe. Drug use and addiction would soar. Hospitals would be filled with many more drug emergency cases. . . . And legalizing drugs would completely undermine the message that drug use is wrong.99

—George W. Bush, "Remarks by the President in Announcement of the Director of the Office of Drug Control Policy."

Opinions about drug legalization vary widely, to say the least. Those who support it are convinced that the results would be overwhelmingly positive: better control, safer drugs, and revenue from taxation that could be funneled into education and rehabilitation programs. This, advocates say, is much preferable to the current system of attempting to fight drug abuse by tracking down and punishing offenders. Ethan Nadelmann, founder and executive director of the Drug Policy Alliance, writes:

What's needed now are conservative politicians willing to say enough is enough: Tens of billions of taxpayer dollars down the drain each year. People losing their jobs, their property, and their freedom for nothing more than possessing a joint or growing a few marijuana plants. And all for what? To send a message? To keep pretending that we're protecting our children? Alcohol Prohibition made a lot more sense than marijuana prohibition does today—and it, too, was a disaster.[16]

The Case for Legalizing Marijuana

Proponents of drug legalization say that if only one drug should become legal, it is marijuana. They often draw comparisons between marijuana and alcohol: While people can and do die from drinking too much alcohol, no one has ever died from a marijuana overdose. In March 2007 a study published in the British medical journal the *Lancet* revealed that alcohol was far more dangerous than marijuana and posed greater risks to society. The research team, led by Professor David Nutt, included drug addiction experts, lawyers and police officers with scientific or medical backgrounds, and doctors. The researchers ranked alcohol as the fifth most harmful drug and marijuana eleventh and determined that alcohol contributed to more than half of all visits to hospital emergency rooms. In their conclusions, the researchers write: "Discussions based on a formal assessment of harm rather than on prejudice and assumptions might help society to engage in a more rational debate about the relative risks and harms of drugs."[17]

> **Proponents of drug legalization say that if only one drug should become legal, it is marijuana.**

Those in favor of drug legalization also question the logic of the justice system's harsh penalties for growing, selling, or possessing even small amounts of marijuana. As Texas journalist Gary Cartwright states: "In America, we spend nearly $8 billion trying to enforce the laws prohibiting the use and possession of marijuana. All we get for our money is a huge increase in organized crime, an endless string of drug-related murders, and the highest incarceration rate in the civilized world."[18] Of the nearly 1.9 million drug-related arrests during 2004, 4.8 percent were for marijuana sale and/or manufacturing and 39.1 percent were for possession. These numbers include more than 6,400 people who were sentenced to federal prison for marijuana-related charges. According to the National Organization for the Reform of Marijuana Laws (NORML), currently as many as 85,000 people in American prisons are there for cannabis-related offenses.

In March 2008 four Missouri men received stiff federal prison sentences after being found guilty of the intent to distribute marijuana. Craig Alan Wansing was sentenced to 8 years and 9 months, Cyrus Pope was sentenced to 7 years and 3 months, David Latham was sentenced to 5 years, and Mark Cavin was sentenced to 3 years. In other states, penalties for marijuana possession are even tougher. In Alabama, for instance, people who are convicted three times of marijuana possession can be sent to prison for life. In Nadelmann's view, this sort of punishment is a result of laws that should not exist. He explains:

> I've had countless conversations with police and prosecutors, judges and politicians, and hundreds of others who quietly agree that the criminalization of marijuana is costly, foolish, and destructive. . . . Marijuana prohibition is unique among America's criminal laws. No other law is both enforced so widely and harshly and yet deemed unnecessary by such a substantial portion of the populace.[19]

Marijuana as Medicine

One of the main reasons many people support the legalization of marijuana is that it has been shown to have medical benefits, such as relieving symptoms of certain diseases and helping to ease the effects of chemotherapy treatments. These benefits have been known for many years. On September 6, 1988, the DEA's chief administrative law judge, Francis L. Young, stated:

> In strict medical terms marijuana is far safer than many foods we commonly consume. For example, eating ten raw potatoes can result in a toxic response. By compari-

son, it is physically impossible to eat enough marijuana to induce death. Marijuana, in its natural form, is one of the safest therapeutically active substances known to man. By any measure of rational analysis marijuana can be safely used within a supervised routine of medical care.[20]

Francis ruled that marijuana be made available to doctors so they could prescribe it as they deemed necessary, but the DEA ignored the ruling and the drug remained illegal.

For people with severe medical problems, smoking marijuana has been shown to provide immediate relief from pain without the unpleasant side effects caused by prescription medication. Patients with Parkinson's disease report that marijuana helps relieve severe tremors and muscle rigidity, while those with multiple sclerosis (MS) or cancer have found that the drug provides relief from pain when other methods have not worked. Cato's David Boaz and Timothy Lynch cite one survey that showed more than 70 percent of cancer specialists in the United States would prescribe marijuana if it were legal, and nearly half said that they had urged their patients to break the law in order to get the drug. Boaz and Lynch also refer to a National Institutes of Health panel, which concluded that smoking marijuana may help treat a number of conditions, including nausea and pain.

> " The researchers ranked alcohol as the fifth most harmful drug and marijuana eleventh and determined that alcohol contributed to more than half of all visits to hospital emergency rooms. "

Although federal law mandates that marijuana is illegal for any use, including medicinal purposes, some states have bypassed federal legislation and passed laws that legalize the drug under certain circumstances. In Rhode Island, for instance, the Edward O. Hawkins and Thomas C. Slater Medical Marijuana Act allows patients with debilitating medical conditions, such as cancer, HIV, and MS, to possess up to 12 marijuana plants and 2.5 ounces (71g) of marijuana. Other states, including California, Colorado, Hawaii, Oregon, and Washington, have passed similar legislation. The state of Alaska went even further in its legalization efforts. In 1975 the state supreme court ruled that adults 19 years of age and older could legally possess small amounts of marijuana for personal use in the home. Although the ruling has been challenged several times and was even repealed in 1988, the original court ruling was upheld in 2006, and marijuana for personal use in the home remained legal.

Yet even in states where marijuana has been legalized for medicinal purposes, people are not immune from federal prosecution if they are caught with the drug in their possession. Kevin Dickes, a veteran of the U.S. Marines who served during the Gulf War, grows and smokes marijuana on the advice of his doctor. When Dickes was stationed in Kuwait during 1991, a grenade exploded near him and severely injured his leg. He now suffers from constant pain, as well as chronic vascular disease, and he possesses a card that allows him to grow and use marijuana for medicinal reasons. But in April 2007, acting on a tip from a neighbor, a team of SWAT officers forced their way into his house in Aurora, Colorado, threw him on the floor, and pointed their guns at him. "They took me down in my own home," he says.

> " Although federal law mandates that marijuana is illegal for any use, including medicinal purposes, some states have bypassed federal legislation and passed laws that legalize the drug. "

"They had guns to my face. I never had that happen to me before, not even in Desert Storm."[21] Dickes was arrested for possession and cultivation of marijuana and taken to jail. In January 2008, however, the charges were dropped and his marijuana plants were returned to him.

The case for medical marijuana was strengthened in February 2008 by a public endorsement from the American College of Physicians (ACP). The large, well-respected physician group released a paper that urged the government to drop marijuana from Schedule I, a category that it currently shares with drugs such as heroin, cocaine, and LSD. The group called for protection of doctors and patients from criminal and civil penalties in states that have adopted medical marijuana laws. After the ACP paper was made public, Marijuana Policy Project spokesperson Bruce Mirken called it "an earthquake that's going to rattle the whole medical marijuana debate." He added that the ACP had "pulverized the government's two favorite myths about medical marijuana—that it's not supported by the medical community and that science hasn't shown marijuana to have medical value."[22]

Does Marijuana Lead to Harder Drugs?

Marijuana is sometimes called a gateway drug, or one that users typically try before moving on to other, more dangerous drugs. Legalization opponents often say that nearly all addicts who use drugs started by smoking marijuana. In December 2006, however, researchers from the University of Pittsburgh Medical Center (UPMC) announced a long-term study that had shown marijuana did not necessarily lead to the use of other substances. The study involved tracking the behavior of 214 10- to 12-year-old boys, all of whom eventually used either legal or illegal drugs. When they were 22 years old, they were categorized into three groups: those who used only alcohol or tobacco, those who started with alcohol and tobacco and then moved on to use marijuana, and those who used marijuana before using alcohol or tobacco (known as reverse gateway). The study determined that marijuana was not the gateway drug that it is often said to be, as UMPC's Susan Manko explains:

> While the gateway theory posits that each type of drug is associated with certain specific risk factors that cause the use of subsequent drugs . . . this study's findings indicate that environmental aspects have stronger influence on which type of substance is used. . . . This evidence supports what's known as the common liability model, an emerging theory that states the likelihood that someone will transition to the use of illegal drugs is determined not by the preceding use of a particular drug but instead by the user's individual tendencies and environmental circumstances.[23]

A major concern of drug legalization opponents is that if marijuana or other drugs were legalized, increasing numbers of young people would become drug users. Even if drugs were only legal for adults to purchase, as alcohol and tobacco products are today, they would still be more read-ily available to children and teenagers whose parents or older siblings had the drugs. In the same way that young people sometimes sneak alco-hol or cigarettes, they might be tempted to do the same thing if drugs were in the house. They might also seek out sources for fake ID cards so they could buy drugs themselves. Judy Guenseth, director of Court Appointed Special Advocates (CASA) of Knox County, Illinois, shares her viewpoint: "There is a great risk in legitimizing marijuana, and once that barrier is down, our country will not be able to rebuild that wall. Taxa-tion will not provide nearly enough revenue to counter the ill effects of increased drug use and most of all it will send a false message of safety to everyone, especially to vulnerable young people."[24]

> "A major concern of drug legalization opponents is that if marijuana or oth-er drugs were legalized, increasing numbers of young people would be-come drug users.

Those who reject the notion that legalization would lead to more young drug users point out that just because drugs are illegal now does not keep them out of the hands of kids. "Schoolchildren can't buy hard liquor," says Cartwright, "but hard drugs are as available as candy on the black market."[25] Yet according to research compiled by SAMHSA, many more young people use alcohol and tobacco products than illegal drugs. In 2006, 32.9 percent of youths aged 12 to 17 reported that they had consumed alcohol during the past year, and 17 percent said they had smoked cigarettes, compared with 13.2 percent who had used marijuana during the past year. These statistics bolster the belief of drug legalization opponents who argue that when drugs are legal, and therefore easier to get, they are more frequently used—and abused—by young people.

One argument that is often made against legalizing marijuana is that the drug is far more harmful and addictive than it was in the past, which increases the risk for young people. Joseph A. Califano Jr., chairman of the National Center on Addiction and Substance Abuse at Columbia Univer-sity, explains: "Today's teenagers' pot is far more potent than their parents' pot. . . . Today, the harmful characteristics of cannabis are no longer that different from those of other plant-based drugs such as cocaine and heroin."[26]

An Uncertain Future

As the debate over drug legalization continues to rage, the only certainty is that the issue is highly complicated and difficult to resolve. Even if more and more states pass legislation that makes marijuana legal, those laws can still be trumped by the federal government. And unless Congress takes the unlikely step of repealing the Controlled Substances Act, marijuana and other drugs are not likely to become legal anytime in the near future.

Primary Source Quotes*

Should Certain Drugs Be Legalized?

66 We hope to one day convince the chiefs of police and others in the law enforcement and criminal justice community that marijuana prohibition simply creates more problems than it solves. 99

—Matt Simon, "Marijuana Ban Failing Just as Prohibition Did," *Concord (NH) Monitor*, January 30, 2008. www.concordmonitor.com.

Simon is executive director of the New Hampshire Coalition for Common Sense Marijuana Policy.

66 The pro-drug lobby masquerades as a champion of individual liberties. But behind that disguise lurks the ugly face of societal decay. Our choice is clear: We can fight the downward spiral into drug dependency, or help it along. 99

—"Drug Legalization Is Not the Solution It's Cracked Up to Be," editorial, *Province*, February 6, 2008. www.canada.com.

The *Province* is a Vancouver, British Columbia, newspaper.

Bracketed quotes indicate conflicting positions.

* Editor's Note: While the definition of a primary source can be narrowly or broadly defined, for the purposes of Compact Research, a primary source consists of: 1) results of original research presented by an organization or researcher; 2) eyewitness accounts of events, personal experience, or work experience; 3) first-person editorials offering pundits' opinions; 4) government officials presenting political plans and/or policies; 5) representatives of organizations presenting testimony or policy.

Primary Source Quotes

66 There are things we can do about drug policy that would reduce the number of people in prison, and the extent of drug abuse and drug related crime. Legalization isn't one of them because there's not public support for it. 99

—Mark Kleiman, "Crime and Punishment," BloggingHeadsTV, February 10, 2008. http://bloggingheads.tv.

Kleiman is a public policy professor at the University of California–Los Angeles School of Public Affairs.

66 In a realistic worldview, substance abuse would be viewed as an expected part of the human condition for some people, an issue with which society would seek the best ways to live with, rather than suppress and 'fight' through the criminal justice system. 99

—David Borden, "Poverty and the Drug Laws," editorial, *Drug War Chronicle*, January 25, 2008. http://stopthedrugwar.org.

Borden is the founder and executive director of the drug reform coordination network StoptheDrugWar.org.

66 As most teenagers will tell you, it is easier for them to buy marijuana than beer or cigarettes. Our marijuana laws don't work. I know it. You know it. Scores of our neighbors know it. 99

—Kathleen Taylor, "Let's Talk About Marijuana," *Seattle Times*, March 18, 2008.

Taylor is the executive director of the American Civil Liberties Union of Washington.

66 This suggestion that because Betty Crocker brand speedballs will be cheaper, purer, and more available, somehow fewer people will ruin their lives taking drugs, seems difficult for me to accept. 99

—Jonah Goldberg, "The Right Dope," *National Review*, February 20, 2001. http://article.nationalreview.com.

Goldberg is an editor at large for *National Review Online*.

66 Who will distribute drugs [if they are legalized]? Government employees? The local supermarket? The college bookstore? In view of the huge settlement agreed to by the tobacco companies, what marketer would want the potential liability for selling a product as harmful as cocaine or heroin—or even marijuana? 99

—U.S. Department of Justice, Drug Enforcement Administration, "Speaking Out Against Drug Legalization," May 2003. www.usdoj.gov.

The DEA is charged with enforcing the controlled substances laws in the United States.

66 By legalizing drugs, the profitability in their sale would evaporate, which would, in one stroke, eliminate everywhere the incentive to grow poppies and thus end the narco-wars in Afghanistan and Columbia . . . [and] would drastically lower the crime rate here and empty out our prisons. 99

—Robert McFarlane, quoted in Gary Cartwright, "Weed All About It," *Texas Monthly*, July 2005.

McFarlane is a cardiologist from Texas.

66 There are more drugs on the street than ever after 35 years . . . and they're more potent, more available and cheaper. If outcome determines success or failure, then we've failed. Do you continue a failed policy, or try something different? 99

—Joel M. Giambra, quoted in Mark Sommer, "Should Drugs Be Legalized?" *Buffalo News*, September 17, 2006. www.mapinc.org.

Giambra is the county executive in Erie County, New York.

❝It is unconscionable for federal agencies to continue to put politically expedient promotion of reefer madness before irrefutable medical science and the will and best interest of the American people. The well-being of thousands of seriously ill Americans backed by the opinion of the vast majority of their countrymen demands that medical marijuana be freed from federal interference.❞

—Valerie Corral, "Testimony of Valerie Corral Before the Subcommittee on Crime, Terrorism, and Homeland Security," July 23, 2007. http://judiciary.house.gov.

Corral is co-founder of the Wo/Men's Alliance for Medical Marijuana (WAMM), a medical marijuana hospice in Santa Cruz, California.

❝The FDA says there's no—zilch, zero, nada—shred of medicinal value to the evil weed marijuana. This is going to be a setback to the long-haired, maggot-infested, dope-smoking crowd.❞

—Rush Limbaugh, quoted in Anthony Papa, "People in Glass Booths Should Not Throw Maggots," *CounterPunch*, May 2, 2006. www.counterpunch.org.

Limbaugh is a conservative radio talk show host.

❝I now understand the pro-legalization viewpoint much better. Although I am still strongly opposed to the notion of drug legalization, I realize that . . . they are Americans, from a broad field, who are truly committed to a cause in which they believe . . . I respect their passion. . . . But they are woefully wrong on this issue.❞

—Edmund Hartnett, "Drug Legalization: Why It Wouldn't Work in the United States," *Police Chief*, March 2005. http://policechiefmagazine.org.

Hartnett is deputy chief and executive officer of the narcotics division of the New York City Police Department.

Facts and Illustrations

Should Certain Drugs Be Legalized?

- In the United States, there were **no legal restrictions** on the importation or use of **opium** until the early 1900s.

- According to the DEA, marijuana's potential for physical dependence is unknown, and its potential for **psychological dependence** is moderate.

- Between 1991 and 2007 illicit drug use among tenth graders rose from **11.6 percent** to **16.9 percent** and among twelfth graders rose from **16.4 percent** to **21.9 percent**.

- According to SAMHSA, nearly **98 million** Americans aged 12 and older have tried marijuana.

- Between 1991 and 2007 cannabis use among tenth graders rose from **8.7 percent** to **14.2 percent** and among twelfth graders rose from **13.8 percent** to **18.8 percent**.

- Of the nearly **1.9 million** drug-related arrests during 2004, **39.1 percent** were for marijuana possession and **4.8 percent** were for sale or manufacturing.

- The Controlled Substances Act regulates **five classes of drugs** in the United States: narcotics, depressants, stimulants, hallucinogens, and anabolic steroids.

Illicit Drugs

Since 1970, when the Controlled Substances Act was passed, drugs have been divided into five separate classes: narcotics, depressants, stimulants, hallucinogens, and anabolic steroids. The following table illustrates some of the most common illegal drugs, as well as information about each.

Drug	Potential for Physical Dependence	Potential for Psychological Dependence	Usual Method of Ingestion	Effects	Effects of Withdrawal
Marijuana (hallucinogen)	Unknown	Moderate	Smoked, oral	Euphoria, relaxation, loss of inhibitions, disorientation, increased appetite	Possibility of insomnia, hyperactivity, decreased appetite
Cocaine (stimulant)	Possible	High	Snorted, injected; smoked (crack)	Increased alertness, exhilaration, euphoria, increased pulse rate and blood pressure	Apathy, long periods of sleep irritability, depression, disorientation
Heroin (narcotic)	High	High	Injected, snorted, smoked	Euphoria ("rush"), drowsiness, constricted pupils, nausea	Watery eyes, runny nose, irritability, tremors, panic, nausea, chills, sweating
Methamphetamine (stimulant)	Possible	High	Oral, injected, smoked	Increased alertness, excitation, euphoria, increased pulse rate and blood pressure, insomnia, loss of appetite	Apathy, long periods of sleep, irritability, depression, disorientation
Ecstasy (hallucinogen)	None	Moderate	Oral, snorted, smoked	Heightened senses, teeth grinding, dehydration	Muscle aches, drowsiness, depression
LSD (hallucinogen)	None	Unknown	Oral	Illusions and hallucinations, altered perception of time and distance	None

Source: U.S. Department of Justice, Drug Enforcement Administration, "Drugs of Abuse," July 2004. www.usdoj.gov.

Who Uses Illegal Drugs

According to the Substance Abuse and Mental Health Services Administration (SAMHSA), people of both genders and all ages and races are drug users, although some groups use them more often than others. The following chart shows the demographic breakdown of people who used one or more illicit drug* at some point during 2006.

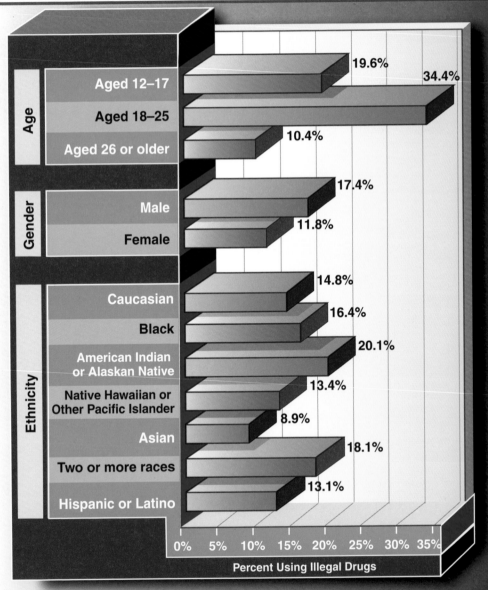

Category	Group	Percent Using Illegal Drugs
Age	Aged 12–17	19.6%
	Aged 18–25	34.4%
	Aged 26 or older	10.4%
Gender	Male	17.4%
	Female	11.8%
Ethnicity	Caucasian	14.8%
	Black	16.4%
	American Indian or Alaskan Native	20.1%
	Native Hawaiian or Other Pacific Islander	13.4%
	Asian	8.9%
	Two or more races	18.1%
	Hispanic or Latino	13.1%

Percent Using Illegal Drugs

*Note: Illicit drugs include cannabis, cocaine (including crack), heroin, hallucinogens, inhalants, and prescription drugs used nonmedically.

Source: "Result from the 2006 National Survey on Drug Use and Health: National Findings," Substance Abuse and Mental Health Services Administration, September 2007. www.oas.samhsa.gov.

States with Medical Marijuana Laws

In 1996 California became the first state to pass legislation that removed state-level criminal penalties for the use, possession, and cultivation of marijuana by patients whose physicians recommended it for medicinal purposes. Since that time, 11 other states have passed similar medical marijuana laws.

November 3, 1998
24 ounces (680g) of usable marijuana, 6 mature plants, and 18 seedlings per patient jointly with his/her caregiver

November 3, 1998
No more than a 60-day supply

November 2, 2004
1 usable ounce (28g) and 6 plants

May 26, 2004
2 usable ounces (57g) and 3 plants, 1 of which may be mature

November 2, 2004
2.5 ounces (71g) and 6 plants, 3 of which may be mature

November 7, 2000
1 usable ounce (28g) and 7 plants, 3 of which may be mature; patients may use affirmative defense to argue that greater amounts are medically necessary

January 3, 2006
2.5 usable ounces (71g) and 12 plants

November 7, 2000
2 usable ounces (57g) and 6 plants, 3 of which may be mature; patients may use affirmative defense to argue that greater amounts are medically necessary

November 5, 1996
Counties can set limits no lower than 8 ounces (227g) of dried marijuana and 6 mature or 12 immature plants; if a doctor's recommendation exceeds that amount, the caregiver or patient may possess an amount consistent with the patient's needs

November 3, 1998
An "adequate supply" means no more than is necessary to ensure an uninterrupted supply for 3 months (defined by the Department of Health as 6 ounces (170g)) of usable cannabis, 4 mature plants, and 3 seedlings

June 14, 2000
7 plants, 3 of which may be mature, and 1 ounce (28g) per mature plant

November 3, 1998
Up to 8 ounces (227g) of dried marijuana and 6 mature or 12 immature plants

WA · MT · OR · NV · CA · CO · NM · ME · VT · RI · HI · AK

Source: "State-By-State Medical Marijuana Laws," Marijuana Policy Project, 2007. www.mpp.org.

How Americans Feel About Legalizing Marijuana

According to an October 2005 Gallup poll, the majority of Americans still do not favor legalizing marijuana—however, the number who support legalization has tripled since 1969, as the following table shows.

Do you think the use of marijuana should be made legal, or not?

Year	Yes, legal (%)	No, illegal (%)	Not sure
1969	12	84	4
1972	15	81	4
1973	16	78	6
1977	28	66	6
1979	25	70	5
1980	25	70	5
1985	23	73	4
1995	25	73	2
2000	31	64	5
2001	34	62	4
2003	34	64	2
2005	36	60	4

Source: U.S. Department of Justice, Bureau of Justice Statistics, "Sourcebook of Criminal Justice Statistics: Attitudes Toward Legalization of the Use of Marijuana," October 2005.

- In 2008 the American College of Physicians recommended that the U.S. government **drop marijuana** from its list of Schedule I drugs.

- Heroin was first synthesized from morphine in 1874; by the early 1900s it was widely **prescribed by physicians** for pain relief.

Would Legalizing Drugs Decrease Crime?

> **❝Drug prohibition creates high levels of crime. Addicts commit crimes to pay for a habit that would be easily affordable if it were legal. . . . When black-market contracts are breached, the result is often some form of violent sanction, which usually leads to retaliation and then open warfare in our streets.❞**
>
> —David Boaz and Timothy Lynch, *Cato Handbook for Congress: Policy Recommendations for the 108th Congress.*

> **❝It is quite likely that violent crime would significantly increase with greater accessibility to dangerous drugs.❞**
>
> —U.S. Department of Justice, Drug Enforcement Administration, "Speaking Out Against Drug Legalization."

How drug legalization could potentially affect crime is a topic of spirited debate. Those who believe drugs should be legalized are convinced that prohibition actually fosters criminal activities because the current drug market is deeply rooted in the violent world of organized crime. Legalizing drugs, they argue, would eliminate the monopoly that the Mafia has over the drug market. As David Boaz and Timothy Lynch explain:

Drug prohibition channels more than $40 billion a year into the criminal underworld occupied by an assortment of criminals, corrupt politicians, and, yes, terrorists. . . . If drugs were legal, organized crime would stand to lose billions of dollars, and drugs would be sold by legitimate businesses in an open marketplace. . . . The immense profits to be had from [the current] black-market business make drug dealing the most lucrative endeavor for many people, especially those who care least about getting on the wrong side of the law. Drug dealers become the most visibly successful people in inner-city communities, the ones with money and clothes and cars. Social order is turned upside down when the most successful people in a community are criminals.[27]

The Connection Between Drugs and Crime

The debate over drug legalization and its connection with crime is not new. For decades people in law enforcement, as well as politicians, economists, journalists, and others, have disagreed about whether legalizing drugs would cause crime to drop or rise. In 1936 former Berkeley, California, police chief August Vollmer wrote the following critique of the way America was fighting its drug problem:

Stringent laws, spectacular police drives, vigorous prosecution, and imprisonment of addicts and peddlers have proved not only useless and enormously expensive as means of correcting this evil, but they are also unjustifiably and unbelievably cruel in their application to the unfortunate drug victims. Repression has driven this vice underground and produced the narcotic smugglers and supply agents, who have grown wealthy out of this evil practice and who, by devious methods, have stimulated traffic in drugs. Finally, and not the least of the evils associated with repression, the helpless addict has been forced to resort to crime in order to get money for the drug which is absolutely indispensable for his comfortable existence.[28]

Today drug legalization advocates say that much of the drug-related crime is the result of users who steal in order to finance their drug habits. In 2006 more than 1.5 million property crimes were committed in the United States, including burglaries, larceny, and motor vehicle theft. If drugs were legal, advocates say, this sort of crime would be markedly reduced because drug prices would drop. Rob English, a man from the United Kingdom, says he was addicted to heroin for 23 years. He speaks about the experience and what he did to finance his drug addiction: "I spent quite a lot of time in prison—I think I went in a total of nine or ten times—because you will do anything to feed your habit. It controls you and you are its servant. You will either resort to crime or do drug dealing because those are the only ways to fund your habit."[29]

> " For decades people in law enforcement, as well as politicians, economists, journalists, and others, have disagreed about whether legalizing drugs would cause crime to drop or rise. "

The DEA acknowledges that people commit crimes in order to buy drugs, but argues that a far greater number of violent crimes are committed by people who are under the influence of drugs. The agency says that more than half of all people arrested in the United States test positive for illegal drugs at the time of their arrest. According to former DEA official Donnie Marshall, people who think drug-related crimes are primarily committed by users looking for money to buy drugs are misinformed. "The fact is," he says, "most drug-related crimes are committed by people whose brains have been messed up with mood-altering drugs."[30] A 2004 survey of inmates at state and federal correctional facilities appeared to support Marshall's contention. Among state prisoners, 32 percent said they had committed their offenses while under the influence of drugs, compared with 17 percent who said they committed their offense to get drugs. There were similar findings among federal prisoners, of whom 25 percent said they had committed their offenses while under the influence of drugs, compared with 18 percent who said they committed their offense to obtain drugs.

Tough Laws and Drug Peddling

Legalization proponents argue that keeping drugs illegal does nothing to reduce the violence related to drug trafficking. When dealers are rounded up and put in jail, others, lured by the chance to earn big profits from drug sales, move in to take their place. Gang warfare becomes the norm as dealers fight over turf, and innocent people are often caught in the cross fire. This is especially a problem in poverty-stricken inner-city neighborhoods.

Former Baltimore police officer Peter Moskos argues that escalating arrests and imprisonments will not change the culture of drug dealers. As long as the demand is there and people want to buy drugs, dealers will continue to sell them. He says:

> While the damage from heroin and cocaine use is real and severe, prohibition creates an illegal market based on cash, guns and violence. While drug use can destroy an individual, the illegal and violent drug trade destroys whole neighborhoods. . . . We need to accept the fact that drug addiction is a personal and medical problem. We need to push violent dealers off the street even if it means tolerating inconspicuous and peaceful indoor drug dealing.[31]

The Impact of Prohibition in 1919

A common argument on behalf of drug legalization is the failure of the Prohibition era, which began in 1919 with Congress's ratification of the Eighteenth Amendment to the Constitution. Prohibition, whose goal was to drastically reduce alcohol consumption and decrease crime, banned the manufacture and distribution of alcoholic beverages in the United States. At the beginning of the movement, the Reverend Billy Sunday shared this optimistic prediction with his congregation: "The reign of tears is over. The slums will soon be a memory. We will turn our prisons into factories and our jails into storehouses and corncribs. Men will walk upright now, women will smile and children will laugh. Hell will be forever for rent."[32]

Yet as much hope as supporters had for Prohibition to transform American society for the better, its effects were far from what they expected. Once alcohol became illegal, organized crime developed rapidly and began to grow in power. Companies that could no longer legally make and distribute alcoholic beverages were driven out of business, replaced by mobsters who were eager to make millions of dollars in the black market. Street gangs began to form, crime escalated, and the prison population exploded, causing severe overcrowding. According to economist Mark Thornton, while violent crime had been declining in the years prior to Prohibition, the homicide rate increased 78 percent during the 1920s. Thornton cites a study of 30 major U.S. cities that showed increases in thefts, burglaries, robberies, and assaults, as well as a significant rise in the number of arrests for drunkenness, disorderly conduct, and drunken driving. Prohibition also became a major contributor to corruption, as Thornton explains: "Everyone from major politicians to the cop on the beat took bribes from bootleggers, moonshiners, crime bosses, and owners of speakeasies. The Bureau of Prohibition was particularly susceptible and had to be reorganized to reduce corruption."[33]

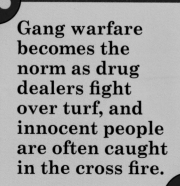

Gang warfare becomes the norm as drug dealers fight over turf, and innocent people are often caught in the cross fire.

In April 1926 New York judge Alfred J. Talley testified before Congress in the National Prohibition Law Hearings, during which he discussed the country's crime situation. Talley said:

> One of the most imposing promises made by the friends of prohibition before the eighteenth amendment was that by abolishing drink crime would be decreased to a minimum. That promise has not been fulfilled. Crime has increased in such amazing proportion that it has become the dominant consideration of most of the State and municipal governments of the Nation. . . . I need not quote statistics to this committee, I am sure, to demonstrate that this is the most lawless country on the face of the earth. I go a step further. I assert that prohibition is one of the largest contributing factors to that disgraceful condition.[34]

In 1933 Congress acknowledged that Prohibition had been a failure, and by the end of that year the legislation was repealed. Not long afterward, crime began to drop and continued to decline throughout the following years.

Those in favor of drug legalization still often refer to the overall failure of Prohibition to stem crime and corruption, and they use it to argue against the Prohibition of drugs. The Drug Policy Forum of Texas says:

> For Americans, the symbol of the drug lord is Al Capone. Prohibition turned him from a young punk in his 20s into one of the most powerful, wealthy men in the world with the power to corrupt police, the judiciary and the electoral process in Chicago. When he went to prison, the illegal alcohol continued without missing a beat. The drug war—modern prohibition—has created the equivalent of a thousand Al Capones and spread them all over the world.[35]

Drug Laws and Crime

Although the government spends billions of dollars each year to fight illegal drugs and continues to sentence many drug offenders to prison, this has not deterred crime. After a 30-year low, crime rates spiked in 2003 and have continued to increase ever since. According to the FBI the total number of violent crimes rose from 597,026 in 2003 to nearly 612,000 in 2006. This, say legalization advocates, is a clear indication that the current approach to fighting drugs is not working. The late Milton Friedman had no doubt that America would be changed for the better if drugs were legalized. In a 1991 interview he candidly explained how:

> I see America with half the number of prisons, half the number of prisoners, ten thousand fewer homicides a year, inner cities in which there's a chance for these poor people to live without being afraid for their lives, citizens who might be respectable who are now addicts not being subject to becoming criminals in order to get their drug, being able to get drugs for which they're sure of the quality.[36]

Those who support drug legalization often point out that police officers' time and talents are being wasted when their highest priority is drug enforcement. If drugs were legalized, police would be freed up to focus their efforts on prevention of violent crime, as well as protecting the United States against terrorism. Boaz and Lynch write: "It is a gross misallocation of law enforcement resources to have federal police agents surveilling marijuana clubs in California when they could be helping to discover sleeper cells of terrorists on U.S. territory."[37]

> **As much hope as supporters had for Prohibition to transform American society for the better, its effects were far from what they expected.**

Another consideration related to law enforcement is that the illegality of drugs has led to widespread corruption. Police officers at federal, state, and local levels have been caught importing drugs, dealing drugs, and accepting bribes to look the other way when drug dealers are caught, as former Seattle police chief Norm Stamper explains:

> As an illicit commodity, drugs cost and generate extravagant sums of (laundered, untaxed) money, a powerful magnet for character-challenged police officers. Although small in numbers of offenders, there isn't a major police force . . . that has escaped the problem: cops, sworn to uphold the law, seizing and converting drugs to their own use, planting dope on suspects, robbing and extorting pushers, taking up dealing themselves, intimidating or murdering witnesses.[38]

One scandal that rocked the Boston police department occurred in 2006, when 3 police officers were arrested for the intent to distribute cocaine. The officers were caught in Miami by undercover FBI agents posing as drug dealers. The following year a 20-year veteran of the Boston Police Department was arrested by federal agents for attempting to extort $265,000 from a man for an alleged debt owed to drug dealers from Colombia.

Can This Issue Be Resolved?

There is no easy resolution to the argument over how drug legalization would affect crime. Some say that legalizing drugs would take the power and control away from organized crime, eliminate the need for street corner drug dealers and their violent turf wars, and result in safer cities and neighborhoods. Others argue that new problems could be created that would be far more severe than what America experiences today. Although there are numerous opinions on both sides, no one knows for sure whether crime would increase or decrease as a result of drug legalization. Many agree, though, that with today's spiking crime rates, increasing drug use, and burgeoning prison populations, something definitely needs to change.

Primary Source Quotes*

Would Legalizing Drugs Decrease Crime?

"By allowing licensed clinics to sell or dispense hard drugs, we could take business away from violent dealers and let rationality and regulated economics rule the streets instead of robbery and murder."

—Jay Hancock, "Making Drugs Legal Not a Fix, Say Ex-Users," *Baltimore Sun*, December 12, 2007. www.baltimoresun.com.

Hancock is a business columnist for the *Baltimore Sun*.

"[Legalizing drugs] cannot change human nature. It cannot improve the social conditions that compel people to engage in crime, nor can it stop people from using drugs as an excuse to be violent."

—Susan Neiburg Terkel, quoted in Edmund Hartnett, "Drug Legalization: Why It Wouldn't Work in the United States," *Police Chief*, March 2005. http://policechiefmagazine.org.

Terkel is the author of the 1991 book *Should Drugs Be Legalized?*

Bracketed quotes indicate conflicting positions.

* Editor's Note: While the definition of a primary source can be narrowly or broadly defined, for the purposes of Compact Research, a primary source consists of: 1) results of original research presented by an organization or researcher; 2) eyewitness accounts of events, personal experience, or work experience; 3) first-person editorials offering pundits' opinions; 4) government officials presenting political plans and/or policies; 5) representatives of organizations presenting testimony or policy.

Primary Source Quotes

❝Legalization of illegal drugs is a worthy pursuit if the intention is to set right our country's unbalanced prosecution of non-violent drug users. . . . But the promise of an end-all solution to crime and other social ills by a large majority of people is not convincing.❞

—Rhonda B. Graham, "Legalizing Drugs Won't End Violence," *Wilmington (DE) News Journal*, December 6, 2007. www.delawarewoman.com.

Graham is a regular columnist for the *News Journal* and a member of the publication's editorial board.

❝Prohibition increases crime and offers obscene profits to drug dealers, builders of prisons, winners of drug wars, and government agencies ostensibly set up to fight the 'war.' The answer is obvious. Re-legalize and regulate drugs.❞

—Dave Doddridge, "American War on Drugs Pits Government Against People," *Lima News*, January 20, 2008. www.limaohio.com.

Doddridge is a former police officer from St. George, Utah, who served for 22 years with the Los Angeles Police Department. He now owns Doddridge P.I., a private investigation agency.

❝Organized crime did not disappear when Prohibition ended in the 20's in the United States; it simply diversified, moving resources and capital into other criminal sidelines. Indeed, legalizing drugs could make the current situation even worse.❞

—Antonio Maria Costa, "Drugs: Cash Flow for Organized Crime," remarks to the Diplomatic Academy, Warsaw, Poland, February 1, 2005. www.unodc.org.

Costa is executive director of the United Nations Office on Drugs and Crime (UNODC).

66 If drugs were legal, they wouldn't be sold on street corners by gangs; they'd be grocery-store commodities. Drug-related homicide—which is to say, the bulk of all homicides—would probably vanish. 99

—Steven Levitt and Stephen Dubner, quoted in Chris Mitchell, "The Killing of Murder," *New York*, January 14, 2008.

Levitt is an economist and Dubner is a journalist; together, they authored the best-selling book *Freakonomics*.

66 After Prohibition ended, did the organized crime in our country go down? No. It continues today in a variety of other criminal enterprises. Legalization would not put the cartels out of business; cartels would simply look to other illegal endeavors. 99

—Drug Free America Foundation, "Myths About the Drug War." www.dfaf.org.

The Drug Free America Foundation is a drug prevention and policy organization that is focused on reducing illegal drug use, drug addiction, and drug-related injury and death.

66 Legalize and regulate all drugs in order to keep our streets safe and our children from being in charge of these dangerous and deadly substances, and to keep our chronically and critically ill off of the streets in search of their medicine. All of our lives depend on it. 99

—Alison Myrden, "Debating the War on Pot," *National Post*, November 26, 2007. www.nationalpost.com.

Myrden is a retired police officer from Burlington, Ontario, Canada.

66 Drugs are the enemy of every family. They're vampires that suck the life out of everyone they attack, and they especially prey on the young. Legalizing them will only force us to remember why we made them illegal in the first place. 99

—Orson Scott Card, "Edwards as Veep; Legalizing Drugs," *Ornery American*, July 4, 2004. www.ornery.org.

Card is an author and professor of writing and literature at Southern Virginia University.

66 In my dream I can walk down any street in Bristol, Boston, Bogotá or Bombay and no one will steal my phone to get their next fix. . . . No crack-crazed youth will kill me for my credit card. And why? Because in my dream they, like me, can walk down that street and buy any drug they like. 99

—Susan Blackmore, letter to the president of the United States, *Edge*, 2003. www.edge.org.

Blackmore is a psychologist and author from Bristol, England.

66 One of these untruths states that prohibition of drugs causes much of the existing violence and therefore generates criminality. If we follow this type of logic . . . we should also legalize such crimes as murder, theft, and rape. Then, they would not be considered crimes, and we would decrease criminality. 99

—Mina Seinfeld de Carakushansky, "Should We Legalize Robbery?" *O Globo* (Rio de Janeiro, Brazil), January 2002. www.drugwatch.org.

Seinfeld de Carakushansky is vice president of Drug Watch International.

66 Many cities, states and even countries in Latin America, the Caribbean, and Asia are reminiscent of Chicago under Al Capone—times 50. By bringing the market for drugs out into the open, legalization would radically change all that for the better. 99

—Ethan Nadelmann, "Drugs," *Foreign Policy*, September/October 2007, p. 28

Nadelmann is the founder and executive directory of the Drug Policy Alliance.

Facts and Illustrations

Would Legalizing Drugs Decrease Crime?

- According to a 2004 survey, **32 percent** of state prisoners and **25 percent** of federal prisoners said they had committed their offenses while under the influence of drugs.

- Between 1997 and 2006 drug abuse violations by female offenders rose nearly **30 percent**, from 155,383 to 201,865.

- Methamphetamine laboratories have been discovered in all **50 states**, with the most in Missouri.

- In a 2007 survey of 500 law enforcement agencies in 45 U.S. states, **58 percent** said that meth is the biggest drug problem, followed by cocaine (19 percent), marijuana (17 percent), and heroin (3 percent).

- Under the auspices of the 1986 federal mandatory minimum sentencing laws, there is a **huge disparity** in the punishment for crack versus powder cocaine; for first-time offenses there is a 10-year mandatory minimum penalty for trafficking 50 grams (1.76 ounces) of crack, while the amount of powder cocaine for the same sentence is 5,000 grams (176 ounces).

- During the 1920s when Prohibition was in effect, the homicide rate increased by an estimated **78 percent**.

- **South Carolina** has the highest rate of violent crime of any U.S. state, surpassed only by Washington, D.C.

Arrests: Drug Abuse Versus Violent Crime

Each year, more people are arrested in the United States for drug abuse violations than for all types of violent crime* combined, and the number of drug-related arrests has markedly increased since 1999. Drug legalization supporters say that law enforcement's time, talents, and energy would be better spent fighting violent crime than tracking down and arresting drug violators. The following illustrates how arrests for these crimes compare.

Year	Murder/Non-negligent Manslaughter	Aggravated Assault	Robbery	Forcible Rape	Total Violent Crime	Drug Abuse Violations
1999	14,920	490,790	109,840	29,220	**644,770**	**1,557,100**
2000	13,227	478,417	106,130	27,469	**625,131**	**1,579,566**
2002	14,158	472,290	105,774	28,288	**620,510**	**1,538,813**
2003	13,190	449,933	107,553	26,350	**597,026**	**1,678,192**
2004	13,467	438,033	108,992	26,066	**586,558**	**1,746,570**
2005	14,062	449,297	114,616	25,528	**603,503**	**1,846,351**
2006	13,435	447,948	125,605	24,535	**611,523**	**1,889,810**

*Violent crime, according to the FBI, includes murder and nonnegligent manslaughter; aggravated assault (including use of weapons); robbery; and forcible rape.

Source: FBI, "Uniform Crime Reports: Crime in the United States," 2008. www.fbi.gov.

- According to the Department of Justice, **50 percent** of the people in American prisons are there because they failed at probation in their communities.

- After a **30-year low**, the number of violent crimes rose from 597,026 in 2003 to 611,523 in 2006.

- According to a 2008 Pew Charitable Trusts report, **1 in 355** white women are incarcerated compared with **1 in 100** black women. The same report shows that **1 in 106** white men 18 or older are incarcerated compared with **1 in 15** black men of the same age group.

Homicide Rate Increased During Prohibition

Prohibition, which lasted from 1919 to 1933 in the United States, was a period during which it was illegal to possess, use, manufacture, or sell alcohol. In making a case against drug prohibition, legalization advocates often point out the effect Prohibition had on crime after it was enacted in 1919. The homicide rate nearly doubled until Prohibition was repealed in 1933, when it began to drop–and by 1943, it was lower than it had been in 1915.

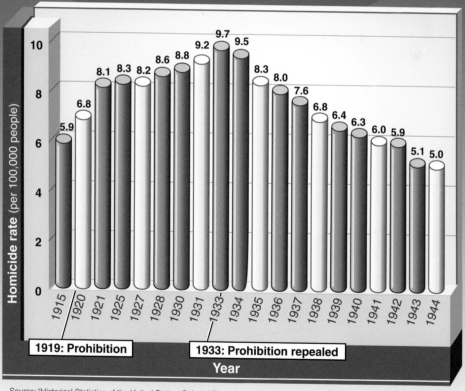

Source: "Historical Statistics of the United States: Colonial Times to 1970," part 1, p. 414, September 1975. www.2.census.gov.

Americans' Concern About Drugs Declining

Americans' opinions about the country's most pressing problems have changed over the years, especially relative to drug abuse. This chart shows how people responded in Gallup polls conducted in 1989 and 2007 when asked the question:

What do you think is the most important problem facing the country today?

	1989 (%)	2007 (%)
Unemployment, job	6	4
Fear of nuclear war; international tensions	2	33
Ethics, morality, family decline	5	6
Crime, violence	6	3
Terrorism	NA	7
Poverty, hunger, homelessness	10	6
Environment, pollution	4	2
Immigration, illegal aliens	NA	11
Drugs, drug abuse	27	1

Source: "Sourcebook of Criminal Justice Statistics," U.S. Department of Justice, Bureau of Justice Statistics, 2007. www.usdoj.gov.

- A study completed in 2000 found that **1.4 million** black men (**13 percent** of the black male population) were unable to vote in the 2000 election because of state laws barring felons from access to the polls.

- The United Nations has estimated the value of the global market in illicit drugs at $400 billion, or **6 percent** of global trade.

Youth Drug Use and Crime

Although there were some fluctuations over the years, illicit drug use among 12–17-year-olds was only slightly higher in 2006 than it was in 1996. This is in stark contrast to youth violent crime arrests, which in 2006 had dropped by nearly 37 percent over 1996. Legalization opponents argue that if drugs were legal, and therefore more accessible to young people, drug use would soar, as would violent crime.

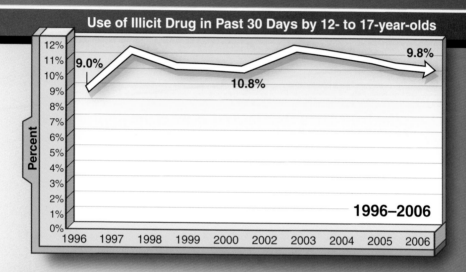

Use of Illicit Drug in Past 30 Days by 12- to 17-year-olds

9.0% 10.8% 9.8%

1996–2006

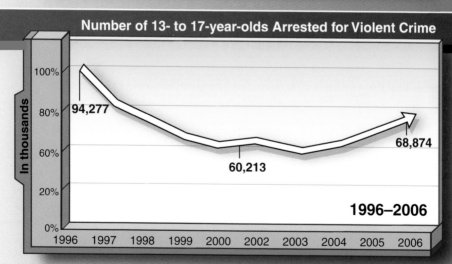

Number of 13- to 17-year-olds Arrested for Violent Crime

94,277 60,213 68,874

1996–2006

*Violent crime includes murder and nonnegligent manslaughter, forcible rape, robbery, and aggravated assault.

Sources: SAMHSA Office of Applied Studies, "National Survey on Drug Use and Health," www.oas.samhsa.gov; FBI Uniform Crime Reports "Crime in the United States." www.fbi.gov.

Would Legalizing Drugs Increase Drug Addiction?

66The effect of drug usage and addiction is not in any way affected by whether or not it's legalized. One only needs to look to history for proof of that.99

—Lieutenant Stan Kid, interview with author.

66The question isn't whether legalization will increase addiction levels—it will—it's whether we care or not. The compassionate response is to do everything possible to prevent the destruction of addiction, not make it easier.99

—"Speaking Out Against Drug Legalization," U.S. Department of Justice, Drug Enforcement Administration.

Of all the arguments against drug legalization, one of the most impassioned is that it would lead to a massive increase in drug addiction. Those who oppose legalizing drugs often use alcohol consumption as a comparison. According to SAMHSA, an estimated 125 million Americans 12 years of age or older are regular alcohol drinkers, compared with 20.4 million who are current users of illicit drugs. If drugs were legal, and therefore as accessible to people as alcohol, the argument goes, the potential for drug addiction could rise dramatically. Former White House drug czar William J. Bennett says that this has already been proven in the past, as he explains: "When powder cocaine was expensive and hard to get, it was found almost exclusively in the circles of the rich, the famous, or the privileged. Only when cocaine was dumped into the country, and a $3 vial of crack could be bought on street corners, did we see cocaine use skyrocket."[39]

Users Versus Addicts

Many legalization proponents argue that just because people enjoy using drugs occasionally does not mean that they abuse drugs or become addicted. Of the 125 million Americans who regularly consume alcohol, only a small fraction are heavy drinkers or alcoholics. So the question asked by drug legalization supporters is, why would the same not be true of casual drug users? Benson B. Roe, a noted heart surgeon at the University of California–San Francisco, says that the number of drug addicts is small when compared with the number of casual users, and the facts are often distorted by people trying to make a case against drug legalization. "The 'demonizers' have focused the public's attention on the small minority of abusers whose conspicuous behavior and disabling complications have serious consequences," he writes, "while conveniently ignoring the millions of drug users who are leading normal, unimpaired, productive lives, as are the majority of those millions who indulge in alcoholic beverages."[40]

Author John Horgan says that he enjoys using psychedelic drugs on occasion. He recalls one instance, after he had finished a particularly stressful project, when he hiked into a forest near his home, pitched a tent, got high on LSD, and spent the day and evening just thinking and writing in his journal. He returned home to his family the next morning feeling refreshed and better than he had for months. "What I did that day should not be illegal," he says. "Adults seeking solace or insight ought to be allowed to consume psychedelics. . . . Recent studies have shown that [they] can be harmless and even beneficial when taken under appropriate circumstances."[41]

> Many legalization proponents argue that just because people enjoy using drugs occasionally does not mean that they abuse drugs or become addicted.

Legalization opponents argue that current drug laws serve as a deterrent to people, even those who choose to use illicit drugs, and this helps prevent them from becoming addicts. Charles VanDeventer, a Los Angeles writer who calls himself a "casual drug user," explains his perspective on this: "The more barriers there are, be they the cops or the hassle or the fear of dying, the less likely you are to get addicted. . . . The road to addiction is just bumpy enough that I chose not to go down it."[42]

Addiction Levels Vary

Even many people who support drug legalization acknowledge that all drugs are not alike, and some are far more addictive than others. One example is crack cocaine, which is one of the most addictive drugs in existence. Texas attorney and business school professor John N. Doggett explains: "The argument for legalization assumes that everyone knows what their tolerance level is. Let me tell you something. Virtually no one can take just a little bit of crack cocaine. If you take crack cocaine, it will take over your life. If you take crack cocaine, you will want even more of it."[43]

According to a February 2008 article in the *New York Times*, growing numbers of young people in Buenos Aires, Argentina, are seriously addicted to a crude form of cocaine known as *paco*. The drug's high lasts no more than a few minutes, but it is so intense that some users smoke as many as 50 paco cigarettes a day in order to make its effects linger. Pablo Eche says that he was addicted to paco from the first time he smoked it, and it nearly destroyed his life. He sold everything he had, committed violent robberies to get cash to buy the drug, smashed his mother's home in a fit of rage, and ended up homeless, alone, and starving. After treatment and rehabilitation Eche was finally free of the drug in October 2007. Today, however, he fears for other young people whose lives may be ruined if they cannot stop using it.

> " Meth also takes a horrible toll on the body, as it causes teeth to rot, destroys tissue and blood vessels, and causes startling premature aging. "

Methamphetamine, which is often called the most dangerous of all drugs, is another highly addictive substance. Like crack, meth has been connected to violent behavior and is linked to a growing number of robberies, burglaries, assaults, and domestic violence cases. People who take meth report a feeling of euphoria that is unlike anything they have experienced before—but once the drug wears off, they become profoundly depressed and many feel the need to keep taking more in order to avoid the crash of withdrawal. Meth also takes a horrible toll on the body, as it causes teeth to rot, destroys tissue and blood vessels, and causes startling premature aging. The skin of meth uses loses its luster and elasticity and often is covered with sores, described by PBS *Frontline* as "the result of obsessive skin-picking brought on by the hallucination of having bugs crawling beneath the skin, a disorder known as formication."[44]

Jeanne Sparks-Carreker, a former meth addict who spent time in an Alabama prison, says she wishes that she could warn others never to try *any* drug for the first time, no matter how non-addictive it is said to be. She is also adamantly opposed to drug legalization, as she explains:

> I battle addiction on a daily basis. Now, years and years after having gotten high that first time, I learn there are certain groups who wish to legalize certain drugs. This is so monstrously insane to me! In the past, I even found myself blaming my country and society for allowing the poison to continue to be in this country and find its way into my life. Could there one day be a way for someone to legally purchase methamphetamine? If that day comes, I hope society is prepared for disaster. . . . Legalizing drugs would definitely recruit more victims into the daily death of drug addiction.[45]

Would Drug Legalization Lead to More Addicted Kids?

One of the biggest fears expressed by legalization opponents is that drug use and addiction among young people would soar. Although adults may be able to make wise decisions about drug use, kids are more impressionable, susceptible to peer pressure, and also highly influenced by advertising. Billions of dollars are spent each year to market alcohol and tobacco products, as well as prescription drugs. If drugs were legal, opponents ask, what would stop manufacturers from creating slick ad campaigns to promote them? That would greatly increase the likelihood that young people would be tempted to use drugs and could potentially become addicted to them. Also, research has shown that the younger people are when they first start to take drugs, the greater their likelihood of becoming addicted. This is especially true with young people who smoke marijuana: The younger they are when they start smoking it, the more likely they are to experiment with other drugs. Mitchell S. Rosenthal, who founded the Phoenix House substance abuse services agency and has worked with addicts for 40 years, explains:

> As parents and policymakers, the vulnerability of teens rightly concerns us most, for the adolescent brain is a work in progress. While the brain's pleasure- and sensation-seeking center is up and running strong at puberty, that portion of the brain exercising control over impulsive and irrational behavior isn't yet fully hooked into the mental communication system until the mid-20s. Lives can be destroyed before they even begin.[46]

Legalization advocates often point out that if drugs were legalized, they would still be illegal for young people to purchase, as is the case with alcohol and tobacco products. Joseph A. Califano Jr. shares his thoughts on this: "Our experience with tobacco and alcohol shows that keeping drugs legal 'for adults only' is an impossible dream. Teenage smoking and drinking are widespread in the United States, United Kingdom, and Europe."[47] Research clearly supports Califano's assertion. According to SAMHSA, in 2006 nearly 11 million youth from ages 12 to 20 said they had drunk alcohol in the past month, 2.4 million of those were heavy drinkers, and more than 3 million young people aged 12 to 17 were current users of a tobacco product.

Drug Policies in the Netherlands

Many who support drug legalization reference countries where drugs are easier to get but their use is no more prevalent than in the United States. In the Netherlands, for example, drugs are illegal but decriminalized, meaning possession or use is not treated as a crime. The country even has establishments known as "coffee shops," which are permitted by the government to sell so-called soft drugs such as marijuana and hashish to customers. Owners of these coffee shops may not sell alcohol or hard drugs, must limit sales to no more than 5 grams (about 0.18 ounces) per person, and are not allowed to advertise their wares. Another requirement is that cannabis cannot be sold to anyone under the age of 18, and minors are forbidden to enter the shops.

> **Many who support drug legalization reference countries where drugs are easier to get but their use is no more prevalent than in the United States.**

Yet even though drugs are easier to obtain in the Netherlands, 5.4 percent of people aged 15 to 64 reportedly used cannabis sometime during the past year compared with 10.3 percent of Americans aged 12 and older. The same was true for cocaine; 0.6 percent of the Dutch population used cocaine compared with 2.5 percent of the American population. There were also fewer current users of LSD and heroin in the Netherlands than in the United States. And for those who are caught violating the country's drug laws, the solution is substance abuse counseling and treatment rather than arrest and prosecution. As a result, about 70 percent of Dutch addicts are in treatment programs, compared with 10 to 15 percent of addicts in America.

"Needle Park" in Switzerland

Switzerland is often a target for criticism by legalization opponents because of its liberal drug policies. Although it is a conservative country, attitudes toward drug use are very different from those of the United States, the United Kingdom, and some other European nations. Between 1975 and 1990, the number of new heroin users in Zurich, Switzerland's most populous city, soared from 80 to 850. During that same time there was also a marked rise in the number of AIDS cases among drug users, which prompted Swiss officials to try a rather unusual experiment. Beginning in 1989 addicts were allowed to buy, sell, or use drugs in Platzspitz Park, located in downtown Zurich. The area became known as "Needle

Park" as thousands of drug users converged on it every day. Health officials freely distributed clean needles, and also provided counseling and advice about available social and medical services.

The park quickly became a magnet for professional drug dealers, and violent crime was rampant. Doggett explains: "Addicts from all over Europe flooded into Zurich. Drug pushers from all over Europe flooded into Zurich. Quickly, needle park became a vomit-covered, needle-strewn wasteland. Violent crime rates soared near needle park. Surprise, surprise, the drug addicts and their pusher suppliers did not stay within the confines of needle park. Slowly but inexorably, needle park polluted much of Zurich."[48] As the problems grew worse and crime rates continued to escalate, city officials closed Needle Park down in February 1992.

Even though the Needle Park experiment failed, drug policies in Zurich have resulted in positive outcomes. Swiss officials have implemented a program that is focused on harm reduction, whereby heroin addicts may visit controlled, medically supervised facilities to obtain clean needles, get heroin injections, and receive methadone or other heroin substitutes. Compared with 1990, when the number of new heroin users in Zurich totaled 850, by 2002 the number had dropped to 150—an 82 percent reduction. According to researchers Carlos Nordt and Rudolph Stohler, who did a long-term study of the Zurich program, its dramatic success shows that such harm-reduction measures are effective. Also, because users must show up at a special facility to get their heroin injections, this has changed the overall perception of heroin use from a "rebellious act to an illness that needs therapy. Finally, heroin seems to have become a 'loser drug,' with its attractiveness fading for young people."[49]

An Unknown Outcome

There is no doubt that drug addiction is a serious, dangerous problem throughout the world. Would it become worse if drugs were legalized? Would it change for the better? Although there is no shortage of opinions on both sides of the issue, no one can say with any certainty how addiction might be affected by drug legalization. Some people strongly believe that the only way to find out is to try it. Others argue that the potential risk is far too great.

Primary Source Quotes*

Would Legalizing Drugs Increase Drug Addiction?

❝We're sick of paying the consequences of this war against drugs with thousands killed each year. People are seeing that if anything things are getting worse, with more people becoming addicts.❞

—Ferney Lozano, quoted in Toby Muse, "Legalization Now! War-Weary Colombia—and Its Conservative Party— Consider Ending the Drug War," *Reason*, June 2005.

Lozano is director of the Legalization Now movement in Colombia.

❝Legalization doesn't change the body's chemistry. Someone addicted to 'U.S. Government Certified Crack Cocaine' will be just as messed up as those addicted to illegal crack cocaine today.❞

—John N. Doggett, "Don't Legalize Drugs," *WorldNet Daily*, March 12, 2008. www.worldnetdaily.com.

Doggett is an attorney and business school professor from Austin, Texas.

Bracketed quotes indicate conflicting positions.

* Editor's Note: While the definition of a primary source can be narrowly or broadly defined, for the purposes of Compact Research, a primary source consists of: 1) results of original research presented by an organization or researcher; 2) eyewitness accounts of events, personal experience, or work experience; 3) first-person editorials offering pundits' opinions; 4) government officials presenting political plans and/or policies; 5) representatives of organizations presenting testimony or policy.

66 **Wouldn't regulated legalization lead to more users and, more to the point, drug abusers? Probably, though no one knows for sure. . . . My own prediction? We'd see modest increases in use, negligible increases in abuse.** 99

—Norm Stamper, "Legalize Drugs—All of Them," *Seattle Times*, December 4, 2005. http://seattletimes.nwsource.com.

Stamper is the former police chief of Seattle and the author of *Breaking Rank: A Top Cop's Exposé of the Dark Side of American Policing.*

66 **The United States has some 60 million smokers, up to 20 million alcoholics and alcohol misusers, but only around six million illegal drug addicts. If illegal drugs were easier to obtain, this figure would rise.** 99

—Joseph A. Califano Jr., "Should Drugs Be Decriminalised? No," *BMJ*, November 10, 2007. www.bmj.com.

Califano is chair of the National Center on Addiction and Substance Abuse at Columbia University.

66 **Drug addiction is a medical problem. There is no political cure for it. . . . Nor is there a criminal justice solution to drug addiction. Locking people inside metal cages does not cure addiction. Sooner or later that addict is going to get out of jail and go right back to the old environment and behaviors.** 99

—Greg Francisco, "Stop Getting Tough on Drugs, Get Smart," letter to the editor, *Times*, December 13, 2007. www.tigardtimes.com.

Francisco, who is from Paw Paw, Michigan, is with the U.S. Coast Guard and is a member of Law Enforcement Against Prohibition (LEAP).

66 **Legalization of cocaine, marijuana, and heroin would lead to large reductions in drug-related crime and mortality, but also to large increases in drug use and addiction.** 99

—Robert MacCoun and Peter Reuter, "Cocaine, Marijuana, and Heroin: The War on Drugs May Be a Disaster, but Do We Really Want a Legalized Peace?" *American Prospect*, June 3, 2002. www.prospect.org.

MacCoun and Reuter are professors of public policy at the University of Maryland.

66 We have all these tough laws and what do we end up with: 5% of the world's population and 25% of the world's prison population, and drug-use rates worse than all those lax European states. Amazing! 99

—Thomas P.M. Barnett, "Foreign Policy's 'Think Again' on Legalizing Illegal Drugs in America," Thomas P.M. Barnett Blog, September 7, 2007. www.thomaspmbarnett.com.

Barnett is an author, a contributing editor to *Esquire* magazine, and senior managing director of Enterra Solutions.

66 Legalization may reduce the profits to organized crime, but it will also increase the damage done to the health of individuals and society. Evidence shows a strong correlation between drug availability and drug abuse. 99

—Antonio Maria Costa, "Free Drugs or Drug Free?" speech given in New Orleans, December 6, 2007. www.unodc.org.

Costa is executive director of the United Nations Office on Drugs and Crime.

66 But will we not die like flies from these addictive substances once they are legalized? There is no more reason to think so than to believe that when the prohibition of booze ended, it encouraged an orgy of drunkenness. 99

—Walter Block, "Drug Legalization: How to Radically Lower the Number of Murders in New Orleans," LewRockwell.com, January 27, 2007. www.lewrockwell.com.

Block is an author and professor of economics at Loyola University in New Orleans.

66 While 'government drugs' could conceivably be priced low enough to eliminate competition . . . the combination of low price and wide availability would result in greater consumption, and consequently increased addiction. 99

—Drug Free America Foundation, "Myths About the Drug War." www.dfaf.org.

Drug Free America Foundation is a drug prevention and policy organization that seeks to reduce illegal drug use, drug addiction, and drug-related injuries and death.

66 Addiction has been an excuse for alarm about these drugs, but that issue too is misleading. Addictions to various substances and activities are numerous. ... And, certainly addiction is not limited to illegal drugs. ... Tobacco is known to be more addictive than heroin, and marijuana is minimally addictive, if at all. 99

—Benson B. Roe, "Physicians and the War on Drugs: The Case for Legalization," *Bulletin of the American College of Surgeons*, October 2001.

Roe is professor and chief emeritus of cardiothoracic surgery at the University of California–San Francisco.

66 This is great talk at 2 A.M. in a dorm room, that all laws should be consistent. But the real world isn't consistent. It's ludicrous to say we have a great deal of problems from the use of alcohol so we should multiply that with marijuana. 99

—John Walters, quoted in Joel Stein, "The New Politics of Pot," *Time*, November 4, 2002.

Walters is the director of the Office of National Drug Control Policy.

Would Legalizing Drugs Increase Drug Addiction?

- The National Institute on Drug Abuse estimates that about **5 million** Americans are addicted to drugs.

- Less than **10 percent** of addicts in the U.S. get treatment.

- According to SAMHSA, **125 million** Americans 12 years of age or older are regular alcohol drinkers, compared with **20.4 million** who are current users of illicit drugs.

- In the Netherlands, where drugs are decriminalized, cannabis users totaled **5.4 percent** of the population aged 15 to 64 in 2005; the number of regular users in America, where drugs are illegal, was nearly double that number.

- According to national drug use surveys, some young people are abusing drugs **before the age of 12**, which means they have a higher likelihood of becoming addicted as adults.

- Cocaine can release **2 to 10 times** the amount of dopamine in the brain as natural rewards, such as a pleasant meal, positive social interactions, or sex, do.

- Injection of drugs such as cocaine, heroin, and meth accounts for **33 percent** of all new AIDS cases and is also a major factor in the spread of hepatitis C.

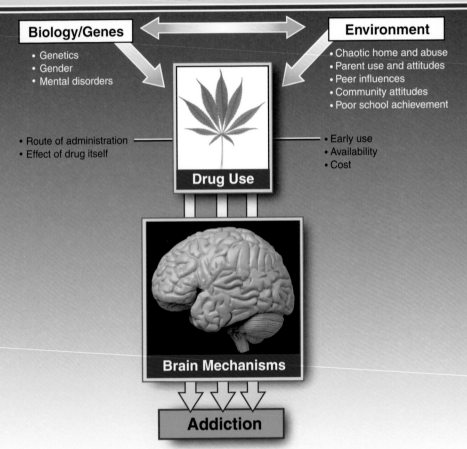

Causes of Addiction

Drug addiction is considered to be a disease of the brain, and as with all diseases, whether people become addicted varies from person to person. According to the National Institute on Drug Abuse, the more risk factors someone has, the greater the chance that taking drugs will lead to abuse and addiction. This chart shows the various risk factors involved.

Risk Factors

Biology/Genes
- Genetics
- Gender
- Mental disorders

Environment
- Chaotic home and abuse
- Parent use and attitudes
- Peer influences
- Community attitudes
- Poor school achievement

- Route of administration
- Effect of drug itself

- Early use
- Availability
- Cost

Drug Use

Brain Mechanisms

Addiction

Source: "The Science of Addiction," National Institute on Drug Abuse, February 2008. www.nida.nih.gov.

- Prescription drugs such as painkillers, sedatives, and stimulants are becoming more prevalent in drug addictions; during 2006 an estimated **7 million** Americans aged 12 and older were regular nonmedical users of prescription drugs.

Heroin Use on the Rise

After heroin was banned in the United States in 1924, the number of regular heroin users dropped sharply. Over the following years, however, heroin use again began to climb. Legalization advocates say that keeping heroin and other drugs illegal has little or no effect on whether people use them or become addicted to them. Heroin use fluctuated from 1979 to 2001, but has steadily risen since then. Its use more than doubled between 2004 and 2006.

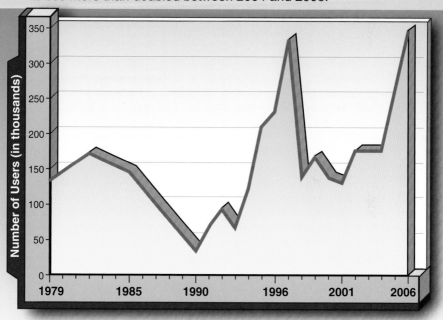

Sources: "Heroin Abuse in the United States," SAMHSA, March 2, 2006. www.drugabusestatistics.samhsa.gov; "Results from the 2006 National Survey on Drug Use and Health: National Findings," SAMHSA, September 2007. www.oas.samhsa.gov.

- There are an estimated **280,000** problem drug users in the United Kingdom and about **2,500** drug-related deaths per year.

- More than **12 million** Americans have tried meth, and **1.5 million** are current users.

- NIDA-funded studies have shown that **prevention programs** involving families, schools, communities, and the media are effective in reducing drug abuse.

Drug Use in Netherlands Versus United States

In its publication "Speaking Out Against Drug Legalization," the Drug Enforcement Administration states that "Europe's more liberal drug policies are not the right model for America." One European country where drugs are illegal but decriminalized is the Netherlands—and as this graph shows, drug use (with the exception of Ecstasy) is markedly lower than in the United States.

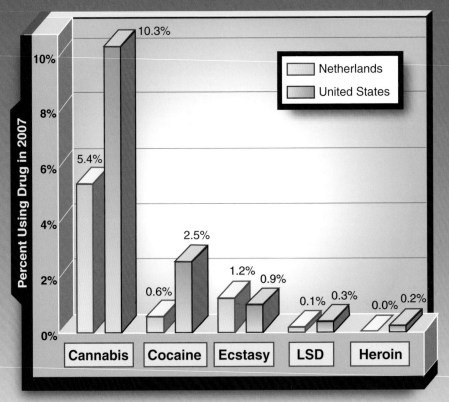

Sources: "Speaking Out Against Drug Legalization," U.S. Drug Enforcement Administration, May 2003. www.dea.gov; "Results from the 2006 National Survey on Drug Use and Health," U.S. Department of Health and Human Services Substance Abuse and Mental Health Services Administration, September 2007. www.oas.samhsa.gov; Margriet van Laarl et al., "The Netherlands: Drug Situation 2007." www.trimbos.nl.

- According to the DEA, when opium was legal in the United States during the late 1800s, there were more than **400,000** opium addicts, roughly twice as many per capita as there are today.

- The DEA says that by 1900, **1 out of every 200** Americans was either a cocaine or an opium addict.

The Most Harmful Drugs

In a study published in March 2007 in the *Lancet*, British researchers proposed that drugs should be classified by the amount of harm they do—and they determined that alcohol and tobacco were more harmful than illegal drugs such as cannabis, LSD, and Ecstasy. They identified three main factors that together determine the harm associated with any potentially abused drug: the physical harm to the individual user; the tendency of the drug to induce dependence; and the side effect of drug use on families, communities, and society. This graph shows the various rankings.

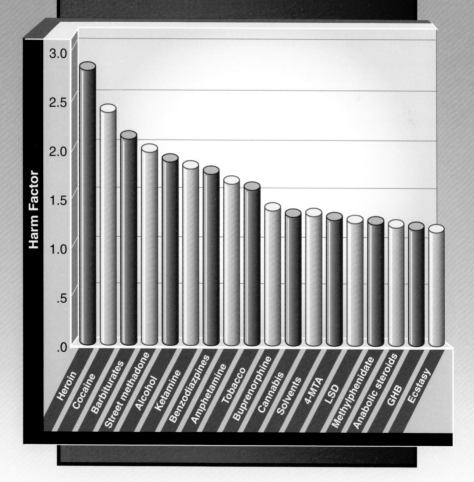

Source: "Alcohol Worse than Ecstasy, According to Proposed 'Matrix of Harm' for Drugs," *Science Daily*, March 225, 2007. www.sciencedaily.com.

Is the War on Drugs Failing?

66 The moralistic drug war has overstuffed our prisons, left communities fatherless, fed corruption, consumed vast quantities of law enforcement time and money . . . all without making drugs scarcer or more expensive. 99

—Bill Keller, "Reefer Madness."

66 We're dismantling drug trafficking operations. We're seizing supplies and we're putting the peddlers of poisons where they belong, and that is behind bars. 99

—George W. Bush, "President Bush Discusses Monitoring the Future Study on Teen Drug Use."

In a March 2008 radio address, President George W. Bush spoke about his administration's drug control strategy and hailed it as a great success. He outlined three components of the war on drugs: disrupting drug supplies by strengthening law enforcement and partnering with other countries to keep drugs out of the United States, using prevention and education programs to reduce the demand for drugs, and providing treatment for those who have become addicted. Bush staunchly defended this approach, saying it had produced measurable results over the years, including a reduction in drug use among teenagers. But many people did not hesitate to disagree; drawing on statistics that show an overall increase in drug use among the general population, escalating crime, and burgeoning prison populations, they insist that the war on drugs is a blatant failure. One particularly outspoken critic is veteran journalist Walter Cronkite, who writes:

> Amid the clichés of the drug war, our country has lost sight of the scientific facts. Amid the frantic rhetoric of our leaders, we've become blind to reality: The war on drugs, as it is currently fought, is too expensive, and too inhumane. But nothing will change until someone has the courage to stand up and say what so many politicians privately know: The war on drugs has failed.[50]

Has the War on Drugs Deterred Drug Use?

In the May 2003 publication "Speaking Out Against Drug Legalization," the DEA cited that overall drug use had declined as a result of the war on drugs. In 1979 an estimated 25.4 percent of Americans were current drug users, compared with 15.9 million in 2001. This dramatic decrease, the agency says, is an example of how effective the drug war has been—yet the numbers have changed since 2001. In 2002 drug users in America 12 years of age or over totaled 19.5 million, and by 2006 the number had climbed to 20.4 million. During that same period the number of marijuana users rose from 11.1 million to 14.8 million, and the number of cocaine users rose from 1.5 million to 2.4 million. Although this is still an improvement over the 1970s, it is an indication that despite tougher drug laws, growing numbers of people continue to use illegal drugs. Even more disturbing is the steep rise in the number of drug-related deaths. In 2000, 15,582 people died as a result of drug dependence, overdoses, or drug poisoning, and by 2005 the number had spiked to 33,541—a 115 percent increase over five years. Those who support drug legalization say that if drugs were legal and regulated by the government, many such deaths could be avoided.

> " In 2002 drug users in America 12 years of age or over totaled 19.5 million, and by 2006 the number had climbed to 20.4 million. "

According to Peter Moskos, history has shown that laws do not deter people's use of drugs; as long as drug users and addicts want drugs, they will always find a way to buy them. He says that the only effective way to lower drug use is to radically change the methods that are in place today and treat drug abuse as a medical problem rather than a criminal one, which would cause drug use to drop. Moskos draws a comparison between illegal drugs and recreational drugs, saying that the policies should be the same. He explains:

> In 40 years cigarette smoking has decreased by half. This is a great victory against drugs. Public education hammered home the harm and changed our culture's attitudes towards tobacco. . . . Few argue that alcohol is an absolute "good." But for the most part people are happy with their localities regulating sales, balancing the rights of individuals with the harm to society. For both tobacco and alcohol, high taxation discourages new users and raises money for education. We should implement similar policies for drug use. Treat drug abuse as a medical problem. Separate the problems of drug use from the violence of the drug trade. Acknowledge that drugs are bad, but don't frame drug policy as a moral war against evil.[51]

A Focus on Punishment

Under the leadership of President Bush, the major focus of the war on drugs was tracking down and punishing drug offenders—but this was not the original strategy of the Bush administration. After the ultra-tough drug policies of the Reagan and Clinton eras proved not to reduce crime or drug abuse, Bush advisors spoke out against harsh sentencing laws in 2001. For example, political scientist John Dilulio stressed that the new administration would take the lead in "reforming drug-related sentencing policies that research had shown were having perverse consequences."[52] Dilulio lamented harsh laws that had put millions of young Americans in prison, denounced the racial imbalances of drug-related arrests, and pledged to focus more heavily on drug treatment programs than punishment.

A year later, when John P. Walters assumed the position of drug czar, the strategy began to change. Walters made it clear that such a program would be far too soft on drug offenders and a tougher approach was the only way to solve America's growing drug problems. He was particularly determined to slash the use of marijuana, as it was the most prevalent drug in the country. He had no tolerance for its cultivation, sale, or use for any reason, including for medicinal purposes. Walters called people who planted and tended marijuana gardens "terrorists who wouldn't hesitate to help other terrorists get into the country with the aim of causing mass casualties."[53] As a result of this tougher, highly punitive approach, arrests for drug offenses began to skyrocket. Between 1980 and 2003 total drug arrests spiked from 580,900 to 1.68 million. In 2006 the number of drug-related arrests totaled nearly 1.9 million—more than for murder, manslaughter, rape, aggravated assault, robbery, and arson combined. According to the FBI, more than four-fifths of those arrests were not for manufacturing or dealing drugs, but for possession.

> " **Walters made it clear that [a treatment-oriented] program would be far too soft on drug offenders and a tougher approach was the only way to solve America's growing drug problems.** "

The massive increase in drug-related arrests and convictions has led to prisons that are crowded beyond capacity. A report titled "Unlocking America" by the JFA Institute states that the prison population rose from 196,429 in 1970 to more than 2 million in 2007. The authors write: "The growth has been constant—in years of rising crime and falling crime, in good economic times and bad, during wartime and while we were at peace. A generation of growth has produced prison populations that are now eight times what they were in 1970."[54] A 2008 report by Pew Charitable Trusts states that an astounding 1 out of every 100 American adults is in prison. Currently there are an estimated 400,000 people in jail or prison for drug-related offenses, with more than 60 percent of the federal prison population consisting of drug offenders. Legalization advocates often cite these statistics as proof that the war on drugs is far from effective and is falling short of accomplishing its goals.

Mandatory Minimums

A major reason that so many drug offenders are in jail or prison today is because of mandatory minimum sentencing laws, which were enacted by Congress in 1986. These laws forced judges to deliver fixed sentences to people who were convicted of a crime, including drug-related crimes. Federal mandatory drug sentences were to be determined by the type of drug, the amount of the drug in possession, and the number of prior convictions, and judges were not allowed to take other factors into consideration. This led to more than an 80 percent increase in the federal prison population between 1985 and 1995. And even though Congress's goal was to target drug kingpins and major trafficking operations, only a small percentage of drug arrests fell into those categories; the majority were low-level offenders or street dealers, with a large percentage being minorities.

Even before the federal mandate was enacted, mandatory minimum sentencing laws were passed by a few states, including New York. One person who received a harsh sentence under that state's mandatory minimum sentencing laws was Elaine Bartlett, a young mother of four from New York City. Bartlett, who was struggling financially, agreed in 1984 to transport a 4-ounce (113g) package of cocaine to Albany, New York, for which she would be paid $2,500. As part of a sting operation, state police caught and arrested her during the transaction, and even though it was her first offense, she was sentenced to 20 years to life in prison. After Bartlett had served 16 years in Bedford Hills Correctional Facility, New York governor George Pataki granted her clemency in 2000, and she was released. During a 2004 interview she said that while she was happy to have her life back again, she was saddened over the loss of 16 years, which took her away from her children. She also shared her feelings about the effectiveness of the current fight against illegal drugs. "The war on drugs is not stopping the drugs from coming into the country; it's not stopped the drugs from getting into our communities, into our kids. The war on drugs, to me, is really a war on families."[55]

> "The massive increase in drug-related arrests and convictions has led to prisons that are crowded beyond capacity."

Is Decriminalization the Answer?

Growing numbers of law enforcement officials, judges, and others are of the opinion that imprisonment is totally ineffective in dealing with nonviolent drug offenders. These people believe that addiction should be viewed as a public health problem, rather than a legal problem. The primary focus, they argue, should be on substance abuse education and treatment instead of punishment. This is the case in the Netherlands, where government officials view drug addiction as a brain disease that requires treatment, not incarceration. Contrary to what many people think, the Netherlands does not have a permissive attitude toward drugs. Although personal marijuana use is tolerated, large-scale drug traffickers are still vigorously prosecuted, as are those who commit drug-related crimes such as robbery. But drug use is not considered a criminal offense, and users are not punished for possession. With these policies in place, not only is the crime rate substantially lower in the Netherlands, the incarceration rate is 100 per 100,000 people, compared with 700 per 100,000 in the United States.

Many people believe the Dutch approach is a more sensible, humane, and effective system than that of the United States, where tough laws often land drug offenders in prison. Research analyst Anthony Gregory shares his perspective:

> Half a million Americans are locked up for nonviolent drug crimes, often under federal mandatory minimums that often put them behind bars for longer prison terms than rapists and armed robbers. This is a major cause of the overcrowded prisons in the United States, which now has the highest per capita prison population in the world. America's Drug War has become an expensive subsidy for violent crime; very few political reforms would do more to reduce violent crime in America than ending it, once and for all.[56]

A Matter of Public Health

In line with America's tough stance on fighting drugs during the 1980s and 1990s, the state of California followed national trends by locking up hundreds of thousands of drug offenders. Between 1988 and 2000, the number of people imprisoned in California for drug possession quadrupled. Seeing this as a trend that was leading nowhere and was not solving the state's drug problems, the Drug Policy Alliance (DPA) helped initiate a piece of legislation known as Proposition 36. Its premise was that drug abuse should be treated primarily as a public health concern rather than a criminal justice concern, and it mandated treatment instead of imprisonment for most nonviolent drug possession offenders.

> " Growing numbers of law enforcement officials, judges, and others are of the opinion that imprisonment is totally ineffective in dealing with nonviolent drug offenders. "

Proposition 36 appeared on the California ballot on November 7, 2000, and voters passed it with more than a 60 percent majority. In a March 2006 report, the DPA states, "Proposition 36 stands out as the most significant piece of sentencing reform since the repeal of alcohol Prohibition."[57] Between mid-2001, when the new program was first implemented, and mid-2005, more than 140,000 people had been diverted from incarceration to treatment programs, and half of them were accessing treatment for the first time. The number of people incarcerated fell by 32 percent, and it was determined that there was no longer a need for the construction of a new men's prison—which saved taxpayers at least half a billion dollars.

One of the people who benefited from Proposition 36 was a woman named Tammy, who had struggled with a heroin and methamphetamine addiction from the time she was just 14. After being in prison twice for drug offenses she was still using drugs, and when she was arrested for the third time, she received Proposition 36 treatment instead of prison. She believes she has her life back because of it, as she explains: "Prop. 36 has allowed me to become a parent again, a daughter, a sister, an aunt, a cousin, a neighbor. . . . I know that if it wasn't for Prop. 36 I would either be in jail or dead right now."[58]

The War on Drugs Controversy

As with every aspect of the drug legalization debate, there are no easy answers to whether the war on drugs is a success or not. On one side are those who insist that the current approach of tracking down users and dealers and putting them behind bars is absolutely necessary and must continue, while others cite the drug war's many failures and insist that the only plausible solution is drug legalization. Even among those who worry that full-scale legalization could be risky and dangerous, more and more people are speaking out to say that the war on drugs is not working and must be overhauled. As journalist Christopher Farrell writes: "As a parent, I find the notion of making heroin or cocaine legally available at the corner liquor store frightening. Yet—with the benefit of several decades worth of hindsight—legalization, taxation, and regulation appear superior to the current strategy of prohibition and prosecution."[59]

Is the War on Drugs Failing?

" When Adam and Eve were living in the Garden of Eden, surrounded by paradise with all their needs met, there was only one thing prohibited to them. Yet, in spite of their perfect existence, they couldn't resist that one temptation. I ask you, if God can't enforce prohibition, what makes us think we can do better? "

—Peter Christ, "Don't Tax Drugs, Legalize Them," *Elmira (NY) Star-Gazette*, February 23, 2008. www.mapinc.org.

Christ is a retired police captain and a founder and board member of Law Enforcement Against Prohibition (LEAP).

" I don't think that you give in to a problem by just acquiescing. I think that there does have to be control and I don't think legalizing drugs is the answer. "

—Gary Delagnes, quoted in Hank Plante, "SF Mayor Gavin Newsom: War on Drugs Is a Failure," CBS Broadcasting, October 4, 2007. http://cbs5.com.

Delagnes is president of the San Francisco Police Officers Association.

66 Marijuana . . . has remained the bedrock of a drug war that has wasted billions in tax dollars, incarcerated millions of people for victimless crimes . . . spawned an international criminal class, and elected countless numbers of witless politicians on a 'get tough on drugs' platform. 99

—John Sperling, foreword to Rudolph J. Gerber, *Legalizing Marijuana: Drug Policy Reform and Prohibition Politics.* Westport, CT: Praeger, 2004.

Sperling is an American billionaire who publicly denounces America's current drug war policies and who has underwritten a state-by-state campaign to decriminalize illegal drugs.

66 Our approach—tough drug laws coupled with effective education programs and compassionate treatment— is having success. It's a great myth that there's been no progress in our anti-drug effort. To the contrary, there's been remarkable success. . . . What doesn't work is legalization. 99

—Asa Hutchinson, "Drug Legalization Doesn't Work," *Washington Post*, October 9, 2002.

Hutchinson is a former U.S. congressman and former director of the Drug Enforcement Administration.

66 Ending the war on drugs will take time, but politicians need to show some backbone. They should do what's best for America and ignore the fringe types who won't be happy until they're again allowed to burn witches. 99

—Gary Cartwright, "Weed All About It," *Texas Monthly*, July 2005.

Cartwright is a journalist from Texas.

> 66 Recent history shows that, far from being a failure, drug-control programs are among the most successful public-policy efforts of the later half of the 20th century. 99

—William J. Bennett, quoted in *Wall Street Journal*, "Don't Surrender: The Drug War Worked Once. It Can Again," May 15, 2001. www.opinionjournal.com.

Bennett is the former director of the Office of National Drug Control Policy and is now the host of *Bill Bennett's Morning in America* radio show.

> 66 The definition of insanity is doing the same thing over and over again, expecting different results. I think the biggest problem is the war on drugs ... we continue to do the same thing. Seventy-four percent of the people agree that the war on drugs is a miserable failure. 99

—Gary Johnson, quoted in Susanna Vagman, "New Mexico Governor Says Drugs Should Be Legalized, Regulated," *Boston University Daily Free Press*, April 18, 2001. www.dailyfreepress.com.

Johnson is the former governor of New Mexico.

> 66 America's drug policy is not, as the critics contend, a dismal failure and a wasted effort. The statistics prove otherwise. 99

—Dan P. Alsobrooks, "Waging a Battle Against Myths," *Corrections Today*, December 2002.

Alsobrooks is a district attorney in Charlotte, Tennessee.

> 66 Since 1981, the United States has spent about as much on its 'war' on all illicit drugs as it did on its real war in Vietnam—some $600 billion to $800 billion in today's dollars. So far, victory has proven just as elusive. 99

—Ken Dermota, "Snow Fall," *Atlantic*, July/August 2007.

Dermota is a journalist in the Washington bureau of Agence France-Presse.

66 America's highly punitive version of prohibition is intrusive, divisive, and expensive and leaves the United States with a drug problem that is worse than that of any other wealthy nation. 99

—Robert J. MacCoun and Peter Reuter, *Drug War Heresies: Learning from Other Vices, Times and Places*. Cambridge: Cambridge University Press, 2001.

MacCoun and Reuter are professors of public policy at the University of Maryland.

66 The thing is that I think we're winning the war on drugs. I think drug use is down. I think if we keep at it, we will win. 99

—John Cooke, quoted in Peter Gorman, "Vets Against the (Drug) War," *Fort Worth (TX) Weekly*, September 28, 2005. www.fwweekly.com.

Cooke is a county sheriff in Greeley, Colorado.

66 Congress and the American people understand that to fail to confront drugs would be to cause a train wreck. 99

—Robert S. Weiner, "The War Is Not Lost," *Washington Post*, August 22, 2007. www.washingtonpost.com.

Weiner is the former spokesperson for the White House Office of National Drug Control Policy and former communications director for the House Committee on Narcotics Abuse and Control.

Is the War on Drugs Failing?

- Since the war on drugs was initiated in the United States in 1971, an estimated **$500 billion** in federal, state, and municipal dollars has been spent to fund it.

- In 2001, **15.9 million** Americans aged 12 and older regularly used drugs; by 2006 that number had risen to **20.4 million.**

- In 2006 the FBI reported that robbery increased **6.3 percent** over 2002, residential robberies increased nearly **13 percent**, and burglaries increased **2.1 percent**.

- In 2000 a total of **15,582** people died of drug-related causes, and by 2005 the number had risen to **33,541**—a **115 percent** increase.

- Between 1970 and 2007 the U.S. prison population grew eightfold, from 196,429 to **2.1 million.**

- In the Netherlands the incarceration rate is **100 per 100,000** people, compared with the United States, where it is **700 per 100,000** people.

- Simple marijuana possession is **no longer a felony** offense in any U.S. state, although some states still issue harsh penalties for it.

Public Losing Confidence in the War on Drugs

The DEA, along with many government officials, insists that the war on drugs is an effective deterrent to the sale and use of drugs and that it should continue. But as this chart shows, participants in an October 2007 Gallup poll seemed to have lost some confidence in the government's progress, compared with responses to polls conducted in 1999. This compares the response when people were asked, *"How much progress do you feel the nation has made over the last year or two in coping with the problem of illegal drugs?"*

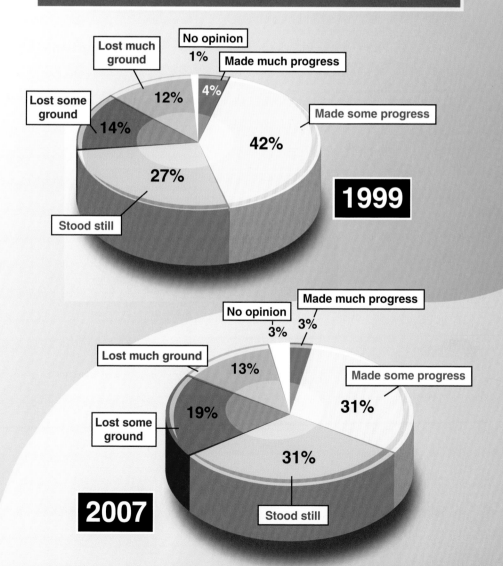

1999

- No opinion 1%
- Made much progress 4%
- Lost much ground 12%
- Lost some ground 14%
- Made some progress 42%
- Stood still 27%

2007

- No opinion 3%
- Made much progress 3%
- Lost much ground 13%
- Lost some ground 19%
- Made some progress 31%
- Stood still 31%

Source: Gallup, "Illegal Drugs," 2008. www.gallup.com.

States with Rigid Marijuana Penalties

Although the possession, cultivation and/or sale of marijuana is against federal law, states set their own guidelines for punishing offenders, and some are much harsher than others. Below are some of the states that have particularly tough marijuana laws.

State	Penalty for marijuana possession	Penalty for marijuana cultivation/sale
Alabama	2.2 lbs (1 kg) or less, 0 to 1 year incarceration, $2,000 fine 2nd offense, 2.2 lbs or less, 1 to 10 years incarceration, $5000 fine	2.2 lbs or less: 3 years MMS*, possible 10 to 99 years incarceration Trafficking: 25 years to life incarceration 2nd offense, MMS life in prison
Delaware	Any amount, 6 months incarceration, $1,150 fine Within 1,000 feet (305 m) of a school, 15 years incarceration, $250,000 fine	Any amount, 5 years incarceration, $1,000 to $10,000 fine
Florida	20g (.71 ounce) or less, 1 year incarceration More than 20g, 5 years incarceration, $5,000 fine	Delivery of 20g or less, 1 year incarceration, $1,000 fine 25 lbs (11kg) or less, 5 years incarceration, $5,000 fine
Louisiana	Any amount, 1st offense, 6 months incarceration, $500 fine 2nd offense, 5 years incarceration, $2,000 fine	Less than 60 lbs (27 kg), 5 to 30 years incarceration, $50,000 fine
Missouri	35g (1.2 ounce) or less, 1 year incarceration, $1,000 fine 35g to 30kg (66 lbs), 7 years incarceration, $5,000 fine	5g (.18 ounce) or less, 7 years incarceration, $5,000 fine 5g to 30kg, 5 to 15 years incarceration, $5,000 to $20,000 fine
Oklahoma	Any amount, 1 year incarceration plus fine 2nd offense, 2 to 10 years incarceration plus fine	Cultivation: 1,000 plants or less, 2 years to life incarceration Sale: less than 25 lbs (11kg), 2 years to life incarceration, $20,000 fine
Oregon	1 ounce to 110g (3.9 ounce), up to 10 years incarceration, $100,000 fine	Any amount, 10 years, $100,000
Tennessee	Any amount, 1 year incarceration, $2,500 fine	Cultivation: 10 plants or less, 1 to 6 years incarceration, $5,000 fine Sale, 1/2 ounce to 10 lbs., 1 to 6 years incarceration, $5,000 fine
Utah	1 oz. to 1 lb, 1 year incarceration, $2,500 fine	Sale: any amount, 5 years incarceration, $5,000 fine

*MMS = mandatory minimum sentence

Source: "State by State Laws," National Organization for the Reform of Marijuana Laws (NORML), August 5, 2006. www.norml.org.

Drug-Related Homicides Declining

The total number of homicides in the United States has significantly dropped since 1993, and as this chart shows, there has also been a decline in the percent of homicides in which drugs were involved. The DEA attributes these sorts of statistics to the success of the war on drugs.

Year	Total Number of Homicides	Percent Drug Related
1993	23,180	5.5%
1994	22,084	5.6%
1995	20,232	5.1%
1996	16,967	5.0%
1997	15,837	5.1%
1998	14,276	4.8%
1999	13,011	4.5%
2000	13,230	4.5%
2001	14,061	4.1%
2002	14,263	4.7%
2003	14,465	4.7%
2004	14,121	3.9%
2005	14,860	4.0%

Source: Tina L. Dorsey, "Drug and Crime Facts," United States Department of Justice, Bureau of Justice Statistics, April 12, 2007. www.ojp.usdoj.gov.

- According to the DEA, **27.9 percent** of drug offenders in state prisons are serving time for possession, and **69.4 percent** are serving time for drug trafficking offenses.

Incarceration: International Comparisons

The United States incarcerates more people than any other country in the world. From fewer than 200,000 in prison in 1970 to more than 2.2 million today, the U.S. prison population has exploded, causing severe overcrowding, the need for additional prisons to be built, and billions of dollars in expense each year for taxpayers. Drug legalization advocates argue that this is one of the failures of the war on drugs: that many people are unnecessarily behind bars for nonviolent "victimless" crimes such as drug possession. This graph shows how the U.S. inmate population compares with the 26 largest European inmate populations. The 26 European countries' inmates total approximately 1.8 million, which is nearly 20 percent less than the U.S. prison population.

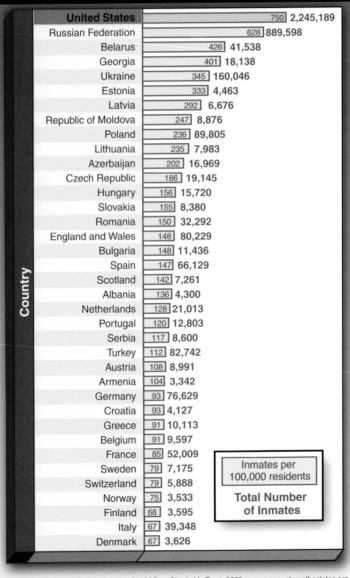

Country	Inmates per 100,000 residents	Total Number of Inmates
United States	750	2,245,189
Russian Federation	628	889,598
Belarus	426	41,538
Georgia	401	18,138
Ukraine	345	160,046
Estonia	333	4,463
Latvia	292	6,676
Republic of Moldova	247	8,876
Poland	236	89,805
Lithuania	235	7,983
Azerbaijan	202	16,969
Czech Republic	186	19,145
Hungary	156	15,720
Slovakia	155	8,380
Romania	150	32,292
England and Wales	148	80,229
Bulgaria	148	11,436
Spain	147	66,129
Scotland	142	7,261
Albania	136	4,300
Netherlands	128	21,013
Portugal	120	12,803
Serbia	117	8,600
Turkey	112	82,742
Austria	108	8,991
Armenia	104	3,342
Germany	93	76,629
Croatia	93	4,127
Greece	91	10,113
Belgium	91	9,597
France	85	52,009
Sweden	79	7,175
Switzerland	79	5,888
Norway	75	3,533
Finland	68	3,595
Italy	67	39,348
Denmark	67	3,626

Source: "1 in 100: Behind Bars in America 2008," Pew Charitable Trust, 2008. www.pewcenteronthestates.org.

- Over **80 percent** of the increase in federal prison populations from 1985 to 1995 was due to drug convictions.

- Between 2000 and 2006 the number of drug offenders sentenced to federal prison rose **26.2 percent**, from 74,276 to 93,751.

- In July 2000 the Portuguese parliament voted to **decriminalize** the use and possession of drugs such as **marijuana, heroin,** and **cocaine;** in doing so, the country joined Italy, Spain, and the Netherlands, all of which have similar legislation in place.

Key People and Advocacy Groups

Harry J. Anslinger: Sometimes called the "father of the drug war," in 1932 Anslinger became commissioner of the newly established Federal Bureau of Narcotics.

William J. Bennett: Bennett was secretary of education under President Ronald Reagan and later held the post of drug czar during the administration of George H.W. Bush.

David Borden: Borden is the founder and executive director of the drug reform coordination network StoptheDrugWar.org and has been instrumental in promoting the use of the Internet to increase awareness of the need to reform current drug policies.

Cato Institute: Cato is a libertarian think tank that is adamantly against any sort of drug prohibition, which it believes is an infringement on the constitutional rights of Americans.

Peter Christ and Jack Cole: Christ and Cole, both former police officers, founded the pro-legalization group Law Enforcement Against Prohibition (LEAP) in 2002.

Drug Enforcement Administration (DEA): The DEA is charged with enforcing all substance abuse laws in the United States.

Drug Policy Alliance (DPA): The DPA is an organization that is devoted to promoting harm reduction rather than punishment for drug offenses and to the overhaul of the current war on drugs.

Ethan Nadelmann: Nadelmann is the founder and executive director of the Drug Policy Alliance and an outspoken critic of the war on drugs.

Richard Nixon: The thirty-seventh president of the United States, Nixon was the first to coin the term "war on drugs" in 1971.

Partnership for a Drug-Free America: This organization is instrumental, especially through its national advertising campaigns, in educating people about the dangers of using drugs.

Mitchell S. Rosenthal: The founder of Phoenix House, a well-known substance abuse services agency, Rosenthal is often called as an expert witness on the subject of drug and alcohol abuse.

John P. Walters: Beginning in December 2001, Walters served as drug czar under President George W. Bush.

Chronology

1900
Heroin is hailed as a nonaddictive treatment for morphine addiction and alcoholism.

1914
The Harrison Narcotics Tax Act is passed, which requires physicians, manufacturers, pharmacists, and others who provide narcotics to register and pay a tax. The legislation eventually evolves into full-scale drug prohibition.

1970
Congress passes the Comprehensive Drug Abuse Prevention and Control Act, of which the Controlled Substances Act is part.

1890
The U.S. Congress imposes a tax on opium and morphine.

1909
In the first act of federal drug prohibition, the U.S. Congress bans the importation of opium.

1933
Alcohol Prohibition legislation is repealed.

1971
President Richard Nixon declares a "war on drugs."

1890 — **1910** — **1930** — **1970**

1906
Congress passes the Pure Food and Drug Act, which is designed to curtail opiate addiction by requiring package labels that state the amount of drugs contained in opium, morphine, and heroin. The American Medical Association approves heroin for medicinal use, but issues caution about its potential to be habit-forming.

1919
The ratification by Congress of the Eighteenth Amendment to the Constitution marks the beginning of Prohibition, which bans the manufacture and distribution of alcohol in the United States.

1968
The Bureau of Narcotics and Dangerous Drugs is founded in the United States.

1972
Nixon signs into law the Drug Abuse Office and Treatment Act and declares that drug use is America's "number-one public enemy."

1895
Heinrich Dreser, an employee of the Bayer Company in Elberfeld, Germany, finds that diluting morphine with chemicals known as acetyls produces a drug without the usual side effects of morphine. Bayer begins production of the drug and names it heroin.

1937
The Marijuana Tax Act adds cannabis to the list of outlawed substances.

Chronology

92

1986

Len Bias, a promising college basketball star, shocks the nation when he dies of a cocaine overdose. The resulting publicity highlights the dangers of cocaine, and drugs become a major political issue. President Ronald Reagan signs the Anti-Drug Abuse Act of 1986, and Congress establishes mandatory minimum sentences for drug offenders.

2006

SAMHSA research shows that the number of drug users in America 12 years of age or older has climbed to 20.4 million, compared with 15.9 million in 2001.

FBI reports show that violent crime in the United States has continued to spike since 2003, with the biggest increases in robbery and aggravated assault.

1973

Nixon establishes the Drug Enforcement Administration (DEA) to coordinate the efforts of all other drug agencies.

1992

Zurich officials close Needle Park.

2001

President George W. Bush appoints John P. Walters as drug czar.

1970   1985   1995   2005

1989

President George H.W. Bush creates the Office of National Drug Control Policy (ONDCP) and appoints William J. Bennett as drug czar.

In an effort to control heroin use and addiction, officials in Zurich, Switzerland, open downtown Platzspitz Park and allow addicts to buy, sell, and use drugs. The area becomes known as "Needle Park," and thousands of addicts and dealers flood the park daily.

2000

California passes Proposition 36, whose premise is that drug abuse should be treated as a public health concern rather than a criminal justice concern.

1993

President Bill Clinton signs the North American Free Trade Agreement (NAFTA), which results in a large increase in trade across the U.S.-Mexican border, making it challenging for U.S. customs officials to detect narcotics hidden within legitimate products.

2008

President George W. Bush presents the 2008 National Drug Control Strategy and praises his administration's success in the war on drugs.

Related Organizations

Common Sense for Drug Policy (CSDP)

1377-C Spencer Ave.

Lancaster, PA 17603

phone: (717) 299-0600 • fax: (717) 393-4953

e-mail: info@csdp.org • Web site: www.csdp.org

CSDP is dedicated to reforming drug policy and expanding harm reduction, a term used to describe programs such as needle exchanges that reduce the risks of drug use, and which CSDP believes are more effective than prohibition. The organization favors decriminalizing the use of hard drugs and advocates that they be available only through prescription. The Web site links to current news articles, "Drug War Facts," a research archive, and the *DrugSense Weekly* newsletter.

Do It Now Foundation

PO Box 27568

Tempe, AZ 85285-7568

phone: (480) 736-0599 • fax: (480) 736-0771

e-mail: info@doitnow.org • Web site: www.doitnow.org

The Do It Now Foundation states that it does not seek to promote a specific political or ideological agenda; rather, to create and disseminate accurate and realistic information about drugs, alcohol, sexuality, and other behavior-related topics. It neither condones nor condemns drug use, but believes it is an individual lifestyle choice unless it interferes with the rights of others. The Web site links to informative pamphlets such as *Straight Talk*, *Street Talk*, *Family Talk*, and *LifeLines*, as well as a Fun & Games section.

Drug Free America Foundation, Inc.

2600 Ninth St. North, Suite 200

St. Petersburg, FL 33704-2744

phone: (727) 828-0211 • fax: (727) 828-0212

Web site: www.dfaf.org

The Drug Free America Foundation is a drug prevention and policy organization that is against drug legalization and permissive drug policies. It seeks to develop, promote, and sustain policies and laws that will reduce drug use, drug addiction, and drug-related injury and death. The Web site offers information about student drug testing and drug policy; a Drug Facts section that covers marijuana, cocaine, heroin, ecstasy, and other substances; current news articles; and recent drug-related studies.

Drug Policy Alliance (DPA)

70 W. 36th St., 16th Floor

New York, NY 10018

phone: (212) 613-8020 • fax: (212) 613-8021

e-mail: info@dpf.org • Web site: www.dpf.org

The DPA states that it believes the war on drugs does more harm than good, and it advocates steps that will reduce the harms associated with drug use. Among the organization's goals are the elimination of criminal penalties for marijuana (except those that involve distribution to children), the repeal of mandatory minimum sentencing for nonviolent drug offenses, the end of incarceration for simple drug possession, and widespread syringe access to reduce the spread of HIV. The Web site links to publications on numerous topics such as the war on drugs, drug policy and the law, facts about marijuana and other drugs, and a blog called The D'Alliance.

Law Enforcement Against Prohibition (LEAP)

121 Mystic Ave.

Medford, MA 02155

phone: (781) 393-6985 • fax: (781) 393-2964

e-mail: info@leap.cc • Web site: www.leap.cc

LEAP was founded in March 2002 by former law enforcement and criminal justice professionals. Its stance is that existing drug policies have failed, and continue to fail, to effectively address the problems of drug abuse (particularly among young people), drug addiction, and crime caused by the existence of the criminal black market in drugs. The Web site links to numerous publications, current news articles, press releases, a community forum, and a blog.

Narcotics Anonymous (NA)

PO Box 9

Van Nuys, CA 91409

phone: (818) 773-9999 • fax: (818) 700-0700

e-mail: fsmail@na.org • Web site: www.na.org

NA is an international organization of recovering drug addicts and has chapters in more than 125 countries worldwide. Its Web site states that NA members meet regularly to help each other stay off drugs. The site links to bulletins, a variety of handbooks, the *NA Way* magazine, and a calendar of events.

National Clearinghouse for Alcohol and Drug Information (NCADI)

PO Box 2345

Rockville, MD 20847–2345

phone: (800) 729-6686 • fax: (240) 221-4292

e-mail: info@ncadi.samhsa.gov • Web site: http://ncadi.samhsa.gov

NCADI is part of the Substance Abuse and Mental Health Services Administration (SAMHSA). The Web site offers educational pamphlets on a variety of drugs, as well as current news stories, research findings, and videos that can be watched online.

National Institute on Drug Abuse (NIDA)

6001 Executive Blvd., Rm. 5213

Bethesda, MD 20892-9561

phone: (301) 443-1124

e-mail: information@nida.nih.gov • Web site: www.nida.nih.gov

NIDA, which is part of the National Institutes of Health, is dedicated to outreach and education initiatives that expand awareness of drug abuse and addiction. The Web site offers a *Marijuana Facts for Teens* pamphlet, as well as a catalog of drug-related publications, news releases, and a booklet that explores addiction titled *Drugs, Brains, and Behavior—the Science of Addiction*.

The Partnership for a Drug-Free America

405 Lexington Ave., Suite 1601

New York, NY 10174

phone: (212) 922-1560 • fax: (212) 922-1570

e-mail: info@drugfree.org • Web site: www.drugfree.org

The Partnership for a Drug-Free America, which is perhaps best known for its national antidrug educational campaign, unites communications professionals, scientists, and parents in an effort to reduce illicit drug use in America. A wide variety of information can be found on the Web site, including research and statistics, current news articles, educational pamphlets, common questions about drugs, and a drug guide with descriptions of drugs, including an alphabetical list by slang names. The site also links to a separate site for teenagers with quizzes, stories, videos, and a message board.

StoptheDrugWar.org

1623 Connecticut Ave. NW, 3rd Floor

Washington, DC 20009

phone: (202) 293-8340 • fax: (202) 293-8344

e-mail: drcnet@drcnet.org • Web site: http://stopthedrugwar.org

StoptheDrugWar.org is a national organization that wants drug prohibition to end and be replaced with programs that are more conducive to regulating and controlling drugs effectively. The Web site contains many news articles, "action alerts," a drug library, and the *Drug War Chronicle* newsletter.

Students for Sensible Drug Policy (SSDP)

1623 Connecticut Ave. NW, Suite 300

Washington, DC 20009

phone: (202) 293-4414 • fax: (202) 293-8344

e-mail: ssdp@ssdp.org • Web site: www.ssdp.org

SSDP is an international grassroots network of students who are convinced that the current war on drugs is failing, yet is still concerned about the impact drug abuse has on communities. It seeks to mobilize and empower young people to push for more sensible policies about drugs. The Web site offers fact sheets, news articles, and press releases, as well as materials that students can download and use in their own campaigns, such as a media guide, sample flyers, brochures, stock photography, and chapter constitutions.

United States Drug Enforcement Administration (DEA)

Mailstop: AES

2401 Jefferson Davis Hwy.

Alexandria, VA

phone: (202) 307-1000

Web site: www.dea.gov

The DEA is charged with enforcing the controlled substances laws and regulations of the United States. The agency investigates and prepares for the prosecution of major drug violators at state and international levels, including criminals and drug gangs. Its Web site offers news releases, speeches, testimonies, and a multimedia drug library, as well as a link to a separate Just Think Twice site for teenagers.

For Further Research

Books

Margaret Pabst Battin et al., *Drugs and Justice: Seeking a Consistent, Coherent, Comprehensive View*. Oxford: Oxford University Press, 2008.

Jonathan P. Caulkins, *How Goes the War on Drugs?* Santa Monica, CA: Rand, 2005.

Paul Doyle, *Hot Shots and Heavy Hits: Tales of an Undercover Drug Agent*. Boston: Northeastern University Press, 2004.

Mitch Earleywine, *Pot Politics: Marijuana and the Costs of Prohibition*. Oxford: Oxford University Press, 2007.

Rudolph J. Gerber, *Legalizing Marijuana: Drug Policy Reform and Prohibition Politics*. Westport, CT: Praeger, 2004.

Doug Husak and Peter de Marneffe, *The Legalization of Drugs: For and Against*. Cambridge: Cambridge University Press, 2005.

Paul Manning, *Drugs and Popular Culture: Drugs, Media, and Identity in Contemporary Society*: Cullompton, Devon, England: Willan, 2007.

David R. Mares, *Drug Wars and Coffeehouses: The Political Economy of the International Drug Trade*. Washington, DC: CQ, 2006.

Robert J. McCoun and Peter Reuter, *Drug War Heresies: Learning from Vices, Times, and Places*. Cambridge: Cambridge University Press, 2001.

Clayton J. Mosher and Scott M. Akins, *Drugs and Drug Policy: The Control of Consciousness Alteration*. Thousand Oaks, CA: Sage, 2007.

Preston Peet, *Under the Influence: The Disinformation Guide to Drugs*. New York: Disinformation, 2004.

Matthew B. Robinson and Renee G. Scherlen, *Lies, Damned Lies, and Drug War Statistics: A Critical Analysis of Claims Made by the Office of National Drug Control Policy*. Albany: State University of New York Press, 2007.

Thomas C. Rowe, *Federal Narcotics Laws and the War on Drugs: Money Down a Rat Hole*. Binghamton, NY: Haworth, 2006.

Rodney Stich, *Drugging America: A Trojan Horse*. Alamo, CA: Silverpeak, 2005.

Steve Sussman and Susan Ames, *Drug Abuse: Concepts, Prevention, and Cessation*. Cambridge: Cambridge University Press, 2008.

Periodicals

Peter Bagge, "The Beast That Will Not Die: Trying to Stop America's Seemingly Impossible 'War on Drugs,'" *Reason*, May 2006.

Joseph A. Califano Jr., "Carrots, Sticks and Children: A Revolution in Drug Policy," *America*, June 4, 2001.

Gary Cartwright, "Weed All About It," *Texas Monthly*, July 2005.

John Cooke, "The Medical Marijuana Debate," *Denver Post*, July 15, 2007.

Ellis Cose, "Sanity and Sentencing," *Newsweek*, December 24, 2007.

Ken Dermota, "Snow Fall: Attacking Cocaine at Its Source Was Meant to Drive Up Prices, yet U.S. Street Dealers Are Selling It for Less than Ever," *Atlantic*, July/August 2007.

Thomas K. Grose, "Abuse as a Disease, Not a Crime," *U.S. News & World Report*, March 26, 2007.

Asa Hutchinson, "Drug Legalization Doesn't Work," *Washington Post*, October 9, 2002.

Gary E. Johnson, "The Case for Drug Legalization: We Need to Make Drugs a Controlled Substance Just Like Alcohol," *World and I*, February 2000.

Claudia Kalb, Tina Peng, and Karen Springen, "And Now, Back in the Real World," *Newsweek*, March 3, 2008.

John L. Kane, "Sheriff Levels Blast at Drug War," *Denver Post*, February 24, 2004.

Corey Kilgannon, "Back in the Saddle, Preaching Drug Legalization," *New York Times*, October 5, 2005.

Alyssa McDonald, "Cannabis: Dazed and Confused," *New Statesman*, November 5, 2007.

Jim McDonough, "A Weed by Any Other Name Smells the Same," *Christian Science Monitor*, December 16, 2002.

Chris Mitchell, "The Killing of Murder," *New York*, January 14, 2008.

Renee Moilanen, "Marihuana: Just Say No Again: The Old Failures of New and Improved Anti-Drug Education," *Reason*, January 2004.

Toby Muse, "Legalization Now! War-Weary Colombia—and Its Conservative Party—Consider Ending the Drug War," *Reason*, June 2005.

Ethan A. Nadelmann, "An End to Marijuana Prohibition: The Drive to Legalize Picks Up," *National Review*, July 12, 2004.

Peter Ninemire, "Treatment, Not Prison: A Case Against Mandatory Sentencing for Nonviolent Drug Offenders," *America*, May 28, 2007.

Christopher Palmeri and Deborah Stead, "'Hands Up and Back Away from the Brownies,'" *BusinessWeek*, August 13, 2007.

Emma Schwartz, "Revisiting the Case of a Sentencing Double Standard," *U.S. News & World Report*, October 8, 2007.

John P. Walters, "No Surrender: The Drug War Saves Lives," *National Review*, September 27, 2004.

Internet Sources

Jorge Castaneda, "Mexico Goes to War: Calderon's Drug Crusade Is Winning Fans, but Can He Win the Fight?" *Newsweek International*, May 28, 2007. http://banderasnews.com/0705/eded-mextowar.htm.

Christopher Farrell, "A New Kind of Drug War," *BusinessWeek*, February 28, 2005. www.businessweek.com/bwdaily/dnflash/feb2005/nf20050228_1996_db013.htm.

Edmund Hartnett, "Drug Legalization: Why It Wouldn't Work in the United States," *Police Chief*, March 2005. http://policechiefmagazine.org/magazine/index.cfm?fuseaction=print_display&article_id=533&issue_id=32005.

Hoover Institution, "Just Say Yes? Drug Legalization" (transcript), August 26, 2003. www.hoover.org/multimedia/uk/2940536.html.

How Stuff Works, "Drugs Channel." http://health.howstuffworks.com/drugs-channel.htm.

Arianna Huffington, "The War on Drugs' War on Minorities," *Los Angeles Times*, March 24, 2007. www.latimes.com/news/opinion/commentary/la-oe-huffington24mar24,1,4064763.story?ctrack=1&cset=true.

John Pickrell, "Drugs and Alcohol: Instant Expert," *New Scientist*, September 2006. www.newscientist.com/channel/being-human/drugs-alcohol/dn9914.

Hilary Shenfeld et al., "America's Most Dangerous Drug," *Newsweek*, October 17, 2007. www.newsweek.com/id/56372?tid=relatedcl.

U.S. Department of Justice, Drug Enforcement Administration, "Speaking Out Against Drug Legalization," May 2003. www.usdoj.gov/dea/demand/speakout/index.html.

Ben Wallace-Wells, "How America Lost the War on Drugs," *Rolling Stone*, December 13, 2007. www.rollingstone.com/politics/story/17438347/how_america_lost_the_war_on_drugs/5.

The White House, "National Drug Control Strategy," February 2006. www.whitehousedrugpolicy.gov/publications/policy/ndcs06/ndcs06.pdf.

Source Notes

Overview

1. U.S. Department of Justice, Drug Enforcement Administration, "Drugs of Abuse," 2005. www.dea.gov.
2. National Institute on Drug Abuse, "Drugs, Brains, and Behavior: The Science of Addiction," February 2008. www.nida.nih.gov.
3. Amy Hughes, interview with author, March 15, 2008.
4. Kailash Chand, "Should Drugs Be Decriminalised? Yes," *BMJ*, November 10, 2007. www.bmj.com.
5. Stan Kid, interview with author, March 1, 2008.
6. Chand, "Should Drugs Be Decriminalised? Yes."
7. A.C. Grayling, "Why a High Society Is a Free Society," *Observer*, May 19, 2002. http://observer.guardian.co.uk.
8. Quoted in John T. Woolley and Gerhard Peters, "Statement About the Drug Abuse Office and Treatment Act of 1972," The American Presidency Project. www.presidency.ucsb.edu.
9. Schaffer Library of Drug Policy, "Harrison Narcotics Tax Act, 1914." www.druglibrary.org.
10. President George W. Bush, "National Drug Control Strategy: 2008 Annual Report," February 2008. www.whitehousedrugpolicy.gov.
11. Quoted in Schaffer Library of Drug Policy, "Interview with Milton Friedman on the Drug War." www.druglibrary.org.
12. David Boaz and Timothy Lynch, *Cato Handbook for Congress: Policy Recommendations for the 108th Congress*, 2003. www.cato.org.
13. Arianna Huffington, "The War on Drugs' War on Minorities," *Los Angeles Times*, March 24, 2007. www.latimes.com.
14. Boaz and Lynch, *Cato Handbook for Congress*.
15. U.S. Department of Justice, Drug Enforcement Administration, "Speaking Out Against Drug Legalization," May 2003. www.usdoj.gov.

Should Certain Drugs Be Legalized?

16. Ethan Nadelmann, "An End to Marijuana Prohibition: The Drive to Legalize Picks Up," *National Review*, July 12, 2004, p. 28.
17. Quoted in Catharine Paddock, "Scientists Say UK Drug Classification Is Flawed," *Medical News Today*, March 23, 2007. www.medicalnewstoday.com.
18. Gary Cartwright, "Weed All About It," *Texas Monthly*, July 2005, p. 86.
19. Nadelmann, "An End to Marijuana Prohibition," p. 28–29.
20. Francis L. Young, "In the Matter of Marijuana Rescheduling Petition," U.S. Department of Justice, Drug Enforcement Administration, September 6, 1988, pp. 58–59. www.druglibrary.org.
21. Quoted in Carlos Illescas, "Veteran Using Medical Pot Fights Arrest," *Denver Post*, June 15, 2007. www.denverpost.com.
22. Quoted in Eric Baily, "Doctors Ask Change in Marijuana Laws," *Baltimore Sun*, February 15, 2008. www.baltimoresun.com.
23. Susan Manko, "No 'Smoking' Gun: Research Indicates Teen Marijuana Use Does Not Predict Drug or Alco-

hol Abuse," University of Pittsburgh School of Medicine, December 4, 2006. www.upmc.com.

24. Judy Guenseth, "Dangers, Costs of Legalizing Marijuana Too Great," *(Galesburg (IL) Register-Mail*, February 8, 2008. www.galesburg.com.

25. Cartwright, "Weed All About It."

26. Joseph A. Califano Jr., "Should Drugs Be Decriminalised? No," *BMJ*, November 10, 2007. www.bmj.com.

Would Legalizing Drugs Decrease Crime?

27. Boaz and Lynch, *Cato Handbook for Congress*.

28. Quoted in Edward M. Brecher et al., "The Consumers Union Report on Licit and Illicit Drugs," *Consumer Reports*, 1972. www.druglibrary.org.

29. Quoted in Jeremy Laurance, "Heroin: The Solution?" *Independent*, June 2, 2006. www.independent.co.uk.

30. Quoted in Edmund Hartnett, "Drug Legalization: Why It Wouldn't Work in the United States," *Police Chief*, March 2005. http://policechiefmagazine.org.

31. Peter Moskos, "Victims of the War on Drugs," *Washington Post*, July 9, 2003, p. A27.

32. Quoted in Mark Thornton, "Alcohol Prohibition Was a Failure," *Cato Policy Analysis*, July 17, 1991. www.cato.org.

33. Thornton, "Alcohol Prohibition Was a Failure."

34. Quoted in Schaffer Library of Drug Policy, "The National Prohibition Law Hearings Before the Subcommittee of the Committee on the Judiciary United States Senate—Sixty-ninth Congress, April 5 to 24, 1926." www.druglibrary.org.

35. The Drug Policy Forum of Texas, "The Drug War: A Record of Failure."

www.dpft.org/failure.htm.

36. Quoted in Schaffer Library of Drug Policy, "Interview with Milton Friedman on the Drug War."

37. Boaz and Lynch, *Cato Handbook for Congress*.

38. Norm Stamper, "Legalize Drugs: All of Them," *Seattle Times*, December 4, 2005. http://seattletimes.nwsource.com.

Would Legalizing Drugs Increase Drug Addiction?

39. Quoted in Hartnett, "Drug Legalization."

40. Benson B. Roe, "Physicians and the War on Drugs: The Case for Legalization," *Bulletin of the American College of Surgeons*, October 2001, p. 18.

41. John Horgan, "Tripping De-light Fantastic," *Slate*, May 7, 2003. www.slate.com.

42. Quoted in U.S. Department of Justice, Drug Enforcement Administration, "Speaking Out Against Drug Legalization."

43. John N. Doggett, "Don't Legalize Drugs," *WorldNet Daily*, March 12, 2008. www.worldnetdaily.com.

44. PBS *Frontline*, "The Meth Epidemic: How Meth Destroys the Body," February 14, 2006. www.pbs.org.

45. Jeanne Sparks-Carreker, e-mail interview with author, April 21, 2008.

46. Mitchell S. Rosenthal, "Sadly, There Is No Magic Bullet," *Newsweek*, March 3, 2008. www.newsweek.com.

47. Califano, "Should Drugs Be Decriminalised? No."

48. Doggett, "Don't Legalize Drugs."

49. Carlos Nordt and Rudolf Stohler, "Incidence of Heroin Use in Zurich, Switzerland: A Treatment Case Register Analysis," *Lancet*, June 3, 2006. www.cesda.net.

Is the War on Drugs Failing?

50. Walter Cronkite, "Telling the Truth About the War on Drugs," *Huffington Post*, March 1, 2006. www.huffington post.com.

51. Moskos, "Victims of the War on Drugs."

52. Quoted in Ben Wallace-Wells, "How America Lost the War on Drugs," *Rolling Stone*, December 13, 2007. www.rollingstone.com.

53. Quoted in Wallace-Wells, "How America Lost the War on Drugs."

54. James Austin et al., "Unlocking America: Why and How to Reduce America's Prison Population," The JFA Institute, November 2007. www. jfa-associates.com.

55. Quoted in PBS *Religion & Ethics*, "Mandatory Sentencing," July 2, 2004. www.pbs.org.

56. Anthony Gregory, "Rolling Back Drug War Crime," The Independent Institute, November 11, 2004. www. independent.org.

57. Drug Policy Alliance, "Proposition 36: Improving Lives, Delivering Results," March 2006. www.drugpolicy.org.

58. Quoted in Drug Policy Alliance, "Proposition 36."

59. Christopher Farrell, "A New Kind of Drug War," *BusinessWeek Online*, February 28, 2005. www.businessweek. com.

List of Illustrations

List of Illustrations

Index

About the Author

Peggy J. Parks holds a bachelor of science degree from Aquinas College in Grand Rapids, Michigan, where she graduated magna cum laude. She has written more than 70 nonfiction educational books for children and young adults, as well as self-published her own cookbook called *Welcome Home: Recipes, Memories, and Traditions from the Heart*. Parks lives in Muskegon, Michigan, a town that she says inspires her writing because of its location on the shores of Lake Michigan.